Stephen
Colbert

Late-Night Comedy Leader

By Allison Krumsiek

Portions of this book originally appeared in
Stephen Colbert by Bonnie Szumski and Jill Karson.

LUCENT
PRESS

Published in 2019 by
Lucent Press, an Imprint of Greenhaven Publishing, LLC
353 3rd Avenue
Suite 255
New York, NY 10010

Designer: Deanna Paternostro
Editor: Melissa Raé Shofner

Cataloging-in-Publication Data

Names: Krumsiek, Allison.
Title: Stephen Colbert: late-night comedy leader / Allison Krumsiek.
Description: New York : Lucent Press, 2019. | Series: People in the news |
Includes index.
Identifiers: ISBN 9781534563285 (pbk.) | ISBN 9781534563261 (library bound) |
ISBN 9781534563278 (ebook)
Subjects: LCSH: Colbert, Stephen, 1964—Juvenile literature. | Comedians–United
States–Biography–Juvenile literature. | Actors–United States–Biography–Juvenile
literature. | Television personalities–United States–Biography–Juvenile literature.
Classification: LCC PN2287.C5695 K78 2019 | DDC 792.702′8092 B–dc23

Printed in the United States of America

CPSIA compliance information: Batch #BS18KL: For further information contact Greenhaven Publishing LLC, New York,
New York at 1-844-317-7404.

Please visit our website, www.greenhavenpublishing.com. For a free color
catalog of all our high-quality books, call toll free 1-844-317-7404 or fax
1-844-317-7405.

Foreword

We live in a world where the latest news is always available and where it seems we have unlimited access to the lives of the people in the news. Entire television networks are devoted to news about politics, sports, and entertainment. Social media has allowed people to have an unprecedented level of interaction with celebrities. We have more information at our fingertips than ever before. However, how much do we really know about the people we see on television news programs, social media feeds, and magazine covers?

Despite the constant stream of news, the full stories behind the lives of some of the world's most newsworthy men and women are often unknown. Who was Katy Perry before she was a pop music phenomenon? What does LeBron James do when he's not playing basketball? What inspires Lin-Manuel Miranda?

This series aims to answer questions like these about some of the biggest names in pop culture, sports, politics, and technology. While the subjects of this series come from all walks of life and areas of expertise, they share a common magnetism that has made them all captivating figures in the public eye. They have shaped the world in some unique way, and—in many cases—they are poised to continue to shape the world for many years to come.

These biographies are not just a collection of basic facts. They tell compelling stories that show how each figure grew to become a powerful public personality. Each book aims to paint a complete, realistic picture of its subject—from the challenges they overcame to the controversies they caused. In doing so, each book reinforces the idea that even the most famous faces on the news are real people who are much more complex than we are often shown in brief video clips or sound bites. Readers are also reminded that there is even more to a person than what they present to the world through social media posts, press releases, and interviews. The whole story of a person's life can only be discovered by digging beneath the surface of their public persona, and that is what this series allows readers to do.

The books in this series are filled with enlightening quotes from speeches and interviews given by the subjects, as well as quotes and anecdotes from those who know their story best: family, friends, coaches, and colleagues. All quotes are noted to provide guidance for further research. Detailed lists of additional resources are also included, as are timelines, indexes, and unique photographs. These text features come together to enhance the reading experience and encourage readers to dive deeper into the stories of these influential men and women.

Fame can be fleeting, but the subjects featured in this series have real staying power. They have fundamentally impacted their respective fields and have achieved great success through hard work and true talent. They are men and women defined by their accomplishments, and they are often seen as role models for the next generation. They have left their mark on the world in a major way, and their stories are meant to inspire readers to leave their mark, too.

America's Comedic Voice

Since the start of recorded history, comedy has been used to tell the truth about nations, leaders, and people's feelings. In kingly courts from the old European empires to early Persian and Chinese dynasties, the fool had an important role. Fools, or court jesters, were clownish figures kept by kings and queens, who would use humor to mock and joke. Because the fool was given leniency by a king or queen, he could deliver bad news about how the people were feeling toward the monarch without fear of punishment. The fool could speak honestly through jokes, songs, and satire without causing offense to the royal who employed him. Part entertainer, part counselor, and part satirical truth teller, a fool could and did become an important member of a monarch's entourage. The monarch often relied on such clever commentary as needed perspective on their rule. In fact, Queen Elizabeth I is said to have been upset with her fool for being too soft with his humor.

Although America has no court, Stephen Colbert plays the nation's fool. Colbert has even used the analogy, calling the character he played for 10 years "a fool who has spent a lot of his life playing not the fool."[1] By good-naturedly mocking (and exposing the hypocrisy of) the media, politicians, and others, Colbert makes pointed commentary on how those in power attempt to both manipulate and win the trust of the American public.

Colbert sheds light on American culture by using comedy.

Thin Line Between Truth and Satire

For decades, as part of an ensemble cast or leading his own show, Colbert has used comedy to poke fun at a vast array of topics—including religion, politics, sexuality, culture, racism, homophobia, marketing, hypocrisy, health, the media, and technology. His blend of satire and concern for America have led him to be one of the leading voices in American television.

For 11 seasons on Comedy Central's *The Colbert Report*, Colbert directed his absurd political commentator persona at every emerging news story. Very few politicians escaped his critical, smart commentary, all delivered with his news anchor personality. When he delivered monologues, Colbert used offensive, outlandish statements to point out the absurdity and offensiveness of people who hold such views. He used deadpan, error-filled observations to make light of the more ridiculous and unbelievable aspects of contemporary society. When he conducted interviews, Colbert could be pure clown, asking absurd questions of his guest. At the same time, he often asked pointed, clever questions that clearly revealed both his level of knowledge on a topic and the lack of critical thinking on the part of his interviewee. This combination of humor and cunning proved a winning combination that entertained as much as it illuminated.

The popularity of his show and his character proves that Americans love and need comedy. Colbert's honors have been serious and prestigious: He has received Emmy awards, Peabody awards, and an honorary doctorate degree from Knox College. He has also received numerous silly honors and fun awards in the pop culture realm. For example, he has his own Ben & Jerry's ice cream flavor, "Americone Dream," and Virgin America airlines

Bennett Cohen (left) and Jerry Greenfield (far right) of Ben & Jerry's Ice Cream are shown here posing with Colbert in 2007 at the launch party for their new "Americone Dream" flavor.

named one of their airplanes after him: Air Colbert. Through the hard work of his fan base, whom Colbert calls the Colbert Nation, he has won national and international contests to rename things after himself.

In 2009, NASA held an online poll to name the new module of the International Space Station. With the help of the Colbert Nation, Colbert's name got 40,000 more votes than the second-place name. Instead of naming the module after him, however, a treadmill on board the space station was named the Combined Operational Load Bearing External Resistance Treadmill, or COLBERT. Colbert's fans are so responsive to his requests, in fact, that the media has called the way they respond to the products and people he promotes as the "Colbert bump." The idea refers to the increase in sales, popularity, or notoriety people or products receive if Colbert promotes them. In this way, Colbert definitely has more than a comedian's influence.

Whether the awards he has received are serious or silly, all serve to show the many ways in which the American public has embraced Colbert as a voice for the nation.

Pop Icon and Political Prankster

Colbert's status as a pop culture icon and his professional persona as a silly prankster mask his quick wit and intellectual approach to comedy. During the *Colbert Report* years, he made sharp observations about American society; he mocked politicians, the political system, corporate America, and the media with such clarity that it was sometimes hard to tell the joke from reality. Colbert's move to late-night network television in 2015 gave him the ability to stop playing characters and be himself on stage. What viewers learned is that the same smart and silly prankster was behind the *Colbert Report* persona the whole time.

At the heart of many of his jokes are smart and fascinating observations about people and deep, philosophical concepts of truth, reason, liberty, and freedom. "Colbert regularly plays around with concepts that are near and dear to the philosopher's heart, concepts such as Truth and Reality," wrote Aaron Allen

Schiller in *Stephen Colbert and Philosophy: I Am Philosophy (And So Can You!)*. "In fact, let me hazard a prediction here and say that from this day forth no philosophical tract on the nature of Truth will be complete without some consideration to the concept of Truthiness."[2] Colbert's ability to call attention to America's philosophical and political struggles in a smart, satirical, and hilarious way makes him one of America's most loved comedians and television hosts.

Joy from Sorrow

Stephen Colbert came from a large and funny family in which knowledge was taken seriously. When Colbert was just 10 years old, two of his brothers and his father were killed in a plane crash. This tragedy greatly shaped Colbert's life and comedy. Afterward, Colbert and his mother were alone together, as his other siblings had grown up and left home. Colbert felt a deep desire to cheer up his mother after the tragedy, and the role of alleviating the sadness of the household would eventually lead to a successful career. Although Colbert's early years were marked by great loss, they were also shaped by a solid, close-knit family deeply rooted in religion and humor.

One of the Family

Stephen Tyrone Colbert was born on May 13, 1964, in Washington, D.C., but he grew up just outside of Charleston, South Carolina. His family's home was located off a dirt road on rural James Island. As a small boy, Colbert took full advantage of the rural lifestyle and enjoyed riding bikes, fishing, and playing with friends. He had an Irish-Catholic upbringing in a large family of 11 children. He was the youngest of eight sons and three daughters.

His father, Dr. James William Colbert Jr., was a doctor of immunology and the vice president of academic affairs at the Medical University of South Carolina (MUSC). Dr. Colbert's colleagues at MUSC spoke highly of him, recalling a gentle man. They also recalled his sense of humor, which may have influenced his son: "The all-too-short time shared at MUSC was memorable for his gifted leadership and unflagging commitment to building a fine academic institution, a goal kept on course by his decisiveness, limitless energy, high integrity and a ready good humor."[3]

An Exaggerated Name

Today, Colbert pronounces his name col-BEAR, although originally, the name was pronounced COL-bert, with a hard t at the end. He debated changing the pronunciation of his name for many years, but it was not until he was on a flight to Chicago, Illinois, to attend Northwestern University's prestigious theater program that he decided to embrace the alternate pronunciation for good. He recalled that his father had given him and his siblings a choice in the matter:

My dad always wanted to be Col-BEAR ... so [he] said to us, "You can be anything you want." And so we made a choice, and it's about half and half. The girls for the most part are like, "Get over it, you're Colbert," but I was so young when this choice was given to us, I think that if somebody woke me up in the middle of the night and slapped me across the face I'd still say Stephen Col-BEAR. But if people don't like what I do on this show, I say, "That's Stephen Col-BEAR, I'm Stephen Colbert."[1]

1. Quoted in Jessie Heyman, "5 Things You Didn't Know About Stephen Colbert," *Vogue*, September 5, 2015. www.vogue.com/article/stephen-colbert-five-things-you-didnt-know.

Stephen's mother, Lorna, was an aspiring actress who set aside her professional ambitions to stay at home and raise her children. Colbert described her as being larger than life. His later theatrical leanings probably started with her—having a witty father and an actress for a mother meant that Stephen was exposed early on to wordplay and role-playing.

Devotion to Faith and Family

Although Stephen's parents were devout, or devoted, Catholics, they allowed for questioning on issues of faith. Colbert said, "I love my Church, and I'm a Catholic who was raised by intellectuals, who were very devout. I was raised to believe that you could question the Church and still be a Catholic."[4] Although they encouraged religious questioning, the Colbert family also had a deep respect for tradition. In a rare description of his upbringing in an interview for *Rolling Stone* magazine in 2009, Colbert recalled a boyhood tradition that carried on to the present day. He said that his family, now numbering more than 50 people with

Colbert and his family are shown here with *Hamilton* actor Jonathan Groff (fourth from left).

nieces and nephews, does a procession through the house on Christmas Eve, lining up from youngest to oldest: "The youngest puts the baby Jesus in the manger on Christmas Eve and we sing 'Silent Night.' It's very traditional."[5]

Though Colbert does not speak often about his early life, he describes his large family of 11 children as very happy. In an interview with Deborah Solomon for the *New York Times*, he once remarked, "I was very loved. My sisters like to say that they are surprised that I learned to walk and that my legs didn't become vestigial [functionless] because I got carried around by them so much."[6] He has sometimes said that his own devotion to his wife and three children is based on the closeness of his upbringing.

Humor was important in the Colbert family as well. He calls his boyhood home a "humorocracy, where the funniest person in the room is king."[7] Colbert was also exposed to the comedy routines of some of the best-known professional comedians of the 1960s and early 1970s. He often listened to comedy albums from comics Bill Cosby and George Carlin. He also appreciated the humor of television variety show hosts such as Dean Martin.

Dean Martin's humor influenced young Colbert.

"A Constant Search for Healing"

Colbert's life changed abruptly when he was 10 years old. On September 11, 1974, his father and two older brothers, Peter and Paul, were killed when an Eastern Airlines plane crashed due to pilot error as it approached Charlotte, North Carolina. Of the 82 people on board, 72 were killed. "Nothing made any sense after my father and my brothers died. I kind of just shut off,"[8] Colbert said. As a result of the tragedy, Colbert became somewhat alienated and detached. He remembers,

> *After they died … nothing seemed that important to me. And so, I had immediately had sort of a, I won't say a cynical detachment from the world. But I would certainly say I was detached from what was normal behavior of children around me. It didn't make much sense. None of it seemed very important.*[9]

Colbert's surroundings changed, too. Soon, his mother relocated the family from James Island to a more urban neighborhood in downtown Charleston, where Colbert found it difficult to make new friends. As he later recalled, "I was not from downtown. I did not know the kids there. I love Charleston … I just wasn't accepted by the kids."[10]

By this time, Colbert's older siblings had already left home or were leaving to attend college, so suddenly, the big, bustling family was reduced to just two: Stephen and his mother. Colbert recalled, "The shades were down, and she wore a lot of black, and it was very quiet. She was a daily communicant [took daily Communion from her priest], and many times I was too. It was a constant search for healing. My mother gave that gift to all of us. I am so blessed to have been the child at home with her."[11]

A Ray of Sunshine in Humor

In his adult years, Colbert has noted how these early hard times helped him develop a sense of humor. It became his mission to make his mother laugh. He has said that people's sense of humor can only be found once they experience great tragedy and lose their childhood happiness. Colbert claims that all comedians have experienced some sort of deep sadness that brought them to comedy in order to cope with it. In his opinion, the development of a comic worldview is deeply rooted in the experience of tragedy.

As he retreated into himself in seventh grade, Colbert began to gravitate toward new pastimes. He became a passionate fan of science fiction, especially books by J. R. R. Tolkien, who wrote *The Lord of the Rings* trilogy and *The Hobbit*. He loved the game Dungeons & Dragons. He said he would play it "every day, if I could find someone to play with me. If I couldn't find someone to play with me, I would work on my player character."[12]

Colbert loved Dungeons & Dragons for many reasons. He enjoyed developing his character because it allowed him to be part of the science fiction and fantasy worlds that he loved and become someone who was adventurous and heroic. He claims that this role-playing was his early entry into acting. The game's complexity gave him a set of rules and constructs that he had to abide by, yet it still allowed him to develop his own character's responses to these predetermined situations. Colbert has argued that the game is the ideal training ground for acting and improvisation.

Finding an Audience

As a teenager, Colbert went to Charleston's Episcopal Porter-Gaud School, where he acted in some school plays but did not excel in academics. At one point, he wanted to study marine biology, but severe inner-ear damage related to complications following surgery to repair a ruptured eardrum ruined these hopes. He became deaf in his right ear and could no longer fulfill the primary requirement for a marine biologist—the ability to scuba dive. Unfortunately, damaged ears make divers unable to equalize the pressure that builds up in their ears during a dive.

By the end of high school, Colbert started to become more social. He dabbled in poetry and recalls writing humorous things for friends: "There was this girl I had a crush on ... so almost

Speaking Like a Newsman

At a young age, Colbert noticed that southerners with thick accents were often portrayed in popular culture as intellectually inferior to those without accents. Colbert described why, despite growing up in the South, he has no noticeable accent:

At a very young age, I decided I was not gonna have a southern accent. Because people, when I was a kid watching TV, if you wanted to use a shorthand that someone was stupid, you gave the character a southern accent. And that's not true. Southern people are not stupid. But I didn't wanna seem stupid. I wanted to seem smart. And so I thought, "Well, you can't tell where newsmen are from."[1]

1. Quoted in Morley Safer, "The Colbert Report," *60 Minutes*, April 27, 2006. www.cbsnews.com/stories/2006/04/27/60minutes/main1553506.shtml?tag=contentMain;contentBody.

every day I would write her a little short story."[13] When he found he could tell jokes and make others laugh, Colbert became even more popular. Between his junior and senior year, he went from being completely unknown to being voted the funniest in his class.

A Classical Education

After high school graduation in 1982, Colbert enrolled in the all-male Hampden-Sydney College in central Virginia. The school's curriculum grounded him in the classics. Colbert said that his two years at Hampden-Sydney taught him to be more disciplined in his academic life. "It was a 'playtime's over' kind of place," he said. "I worked very hard … I didn't have the self-discipline, so it took a lot more time to do the work … You had to finish classes, come back to your room, and immediately start working."[14]

Hampden-Sydney was very old-fashioned and conservative. Colbert describes it as like going to school more than 100 years ago. He took classes in rhetoric (discourse, or speech), read classic books, studied Western civilization, and was expected to follow the school's strict honor code. As Colbert said, it was a "very regimented curriculum, and a 19th-century emphasis on rhetoric and grammar—and all male."[15] Hampden-Sydney was where Colbert began to take performing seriously. His theater professor, Steve Coy, encouraged him. Coy was more open to unconventional ideas, and his personality struck a chord with Colbert.

During this period, Colbert performed in the farce *Oh Dad, Poor Dad, Mamma's Hung You in the Closet and I'm Feelin' So Sad* by playwright Arthur Kopit. The play's plot involves a woman vacationing in a Caribbean resort with her son and dead husband, whose body she brings along in a casket and whose voice serves as the narrator. Colbert loved the dark theme of the play, especially the absurdity of the dialogue. He was impressed that the actors could say interesting things in the play in such a way as to make the audience laugh.

Taking to the Stage

In 1984, after two years at Hampden-Sydney, Colbert transferred to Northwestern University in Chicago, Illinois, to major in theater. There he enjoyed a much more liberal environment. Colbert attributes wanting to change colleges to an even more serious desire to perform. He decided that theater was his passion and the only thing he was interested in studying.

Colbert initially planned to pursue a dramatic acting career. He studied the great plays, including the works of William Shakespeare and George Bernard Shaw, for that purpose. He said, "I meant to be a serious actor with a beard who wore a lot of black and wanted to share his misery with you."[16]

The program at Northwestern was very intense. Colbert's theater training included classes in other performing arts, such as dance, as well as working on theater productions in set design and as a member of the production crew. His academic requirements included courses in drama criticism, the history of theater, and the history of costume and décor. The days were long; he often worked from early morning until late at night. Colbert recalls that his fellow classmates were just as dedicated as he was. It was the first time that he was immersed in an environment where everyone was equally devoted to theater.

Shown here is Northwestern University, where Colbert studied classical theater, including Shakespeare.

Formation of Character

During the next few years at Northwestern, Colbert discovered a love of improvisational comedy, which is comedy that is done without preparation. Just as important, he started to develop the character that would one day make him famous.

A number of former classmates at Northwestern trace the genesis of the ridiculous but lovable news character that Colbert eventually became known for back to specific roles performed during his Northwestern years. For example, in the school's production of *Terry Won't Talk*, Colbert played the role of a high school principal. According to playwright and director Aaron Posner, who was one of Colbert's classmates at Northwestern, the character was "very much a cigar-chomping, blue-blazered, high-status idiot. [Colbert] could play fairly reprehensible [bad] people in a way that you still really liked them."[17]

In another example, Colbert and a group of classmates and other colleagues formed the Journeymen Theater Ensemble. This troop performed *Rumpelstiltskin v. the Queen* and other plays at schools in the surrounding areas. In the *Rumpelstiltskin* production, Colbert played the role of the miller. Classmates assert that Colbert's most famous character is particularly reminiscent of this role, as young Colbert's miller was self-important and overblown.

The Second City

Even though he loved formal theater, Colbert soon discovered a love of improvisational comedy after watching improvisation teams at a comedy club in Chicago. In improvisation, actors often come up with an idea for a scene and the characters within it, but all dialogue is made up on the spot. Colbert recalls how he felt compelled to participate in this form of comedy: "I just loved going onstage with nothing planned."[18] Soon after, Stephen began performing with Northwestern's improvisation team, which was called the No Fun Mud Piranhas. He also performed comedy at iO, formerly ImprovOlympic, at Chicago's Annoyance Theater. Many up-and-coming comedians also did improv at iO, including Mike Myers, Chris Farley, and Tina Fey.

As his improvisation career took root, Colbert started to relinquish his dream of serious, dramatic acting, dedicating himself instead to improvisation. A friend who performed with Colbert said, "Speaking somebody else's words wasn't as exciting for him as creating on the fly on his own."[19]

Colbert completed Northwestern's three-year theater program in two years. After he graduated in 1986, he took a job at the

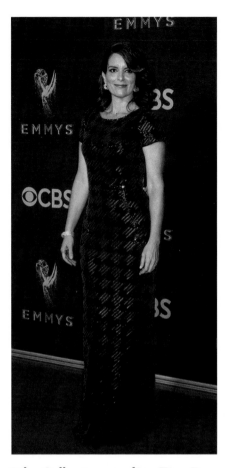

Like Colbert, comedian Tina Fey performed improvisational comedy in Chicago.

box office at The Second City, a comedy school and performance nightclub in Chicago. The school and club are famous for premiering comics who go on to become huge stars. Because he was employed there, Colbert was able to take improvisation classes at Second City's training center for free. He auditioned to perform with Second City's touring company and was hired on the same day as several other budding comedians, including Amy Sedaris, Paul Dinello, Scott Allman, and Chris Farley. Colbert was thrilled. Among his talented colleagues was a young comedic actor named Steve Carell. Colbert was Carell's understudy, which meant he was the one who took Carell's place on stage when Carell could not perform.

Colbert later described a particular moment with The Second City that made his transition from drama to comedy complete:

I saw someone fail onstage—terribly, massively fail onstage … And we backstage laughed so hard at this woman's failure, and our laughter was so joyful and not derisive … And I thought, "This is healthier than straight theater." Because in straight theater when someone fails, you come backstage, and people are very quietly sort of touching up their makeup, going, "How's it

Husband and Father

Today, Colbert is married to Evelyn McGee-Colbert and they have three children together—Madeline, Peter, and John. The couple first met in 1990. At the time, Colbert had a girlfriend who was pressing him to get married. Colbert returned to his hometown of Charleston to contemplate this important decision. While home, his mother took him to a show, where he met McGee. Colbert describes this first meeting as love at first sight: "I'll never forget it. I walk in and I see this woman across the lobby and I thought, 'That one. Right there.' At that moment, I thought, 'That's crazy. You're crazy, Colbert.' And it turned out I was right."[1] He spent the entire evening talking to her, and they were married in 1993. In a 2017 interview with Humans of New York, Evelyn said of her husband of nearly 25 years, "He taught me the importance of being silly."[2]

Colbert is also a loving, devoted father. He has stated in the past that he rarely allowed his three children to watch his show: "I say things in a very flat manner that

going out there? It seems pretty quiet." … That is the moment when I said, "I will do this and not drama, I will do comedy and not drama," and never turned back.[20]

Comedy on TV

In the early 1990s, at the end of his stint at The Second City, Colbert moved to New York with Sedaris and Dinello. Together, they developed *Exit 57*, a television comedy series that debuted on Comedy Central in 1995. Although the show was canceled after only 12 episodes, it received good reviews and was

"I don't believe, and I don't want them to perceive Daddy as insincere ... I basically tell them I'm professionally ridiculous."[3]

1. Quoted in Bryce Donovan, "Great Charlestonian? Or the Greatest Charlestonian? Stephen Colbert," *Post and Courier*, April 29, 2006. www.postandcourier.com/stories/?newsID=83674.

2. Humans of New York (@ humansofnewyork), Facebook, May 2, 2017. www.facebook.com/humansofnewyork/posts/1711528725587887:0.

3. Quoted in Marc Peyser, "The Truthiness Teller," *Newsweek*, February 12, 2006. www.newsweek.com/2006/02/12/the-truthiness-teller.html.

Colbert and his wife, Evelyn, are shown here at a gala at the Metropolitan Museum of Art in 2016.

nominated for several CableACE awards in the categories of best actress and best comedy series. Colbert recalls that budgets were extremely tight on the short-lived show—the actors would think up great sketches but were not always able to afford the necessary props. Colbert gave an example of how the show's development would go: "'Well, here's an idea. A guy gets woken up by a jackhammer. The jackhammer operator ...' and our producers would say, 'First of all, before you go any further—do you have a jackhammer? Because I don't have a jackhammer.'"[21]

Colbert went on to work with Steve Carell and others as a cast member and writer on the ABC comedy sketch show *The Dana Carvey Show*, a vehicle for *Saturday Night Live (SNL)* star Dana Carvey that was canceled after only eight episodes. Sponsors pulled out after the show was described as being of questionable taste. After another failure to secure permanent work, Colbert worried that paying his bills would become a struggle. He was married and had one small child at the time, and he needed to think seriously about how to support his young family.

Colbert took work wherever he could find it, writing bits for other shows, including *SNL*. Working with *SNL* comedian Robert Smigel, with whom he had worked on *The Dana Carvey Show*, Colbert cowrote and coproduced recurring *SNL* cartoons. Colbert began to develop character voices while working on these cartoons for *SNL* with Carell.

To pay the bills, Colbert also took a job filming humorous segments for the ABC morning news and talk show *Good Morning America*. Although it was paid work, something he desperately needed at the time, he did not enjoy the restrictions of the format. Although only one segment ever aired, his stint at *Good Morning America* captured the attention of Madeleine Smithberg, who was at that time the producer of a comedy show called *The Daily Show*.

First Sweet Break

Around this time, Colbert teamed up once again with fellow comedians Amy Sedaris and Paul Dinello. The trio developed the Comedy Central series *Strangers with Candy*, which would go on to become a cult classic (a movie or TV show that is popular among a particular audience). The show was meant to parody after-school specials. These specials, more like soap operas for teenagers, generally took place in a school setting and featured teen characters in trouble. *Strangers with Candy* told the story of 46-year-old high school dropout Jerri Blank, who returns to finish school after more than 30 years of homelessness and drug addiction.

Colbert played Chuck Noblet, a strict but uninformed history teacher who delivers questionable—and often absurd—lessons to his students. In one episode, for example, Noblet had this

The cast of *Strangers with Candy* is shown here (clockwise): Stephen Colbert, Chris Pratt, Paul Dinello, and Amy Sedaris.

conversation with another teacher:

> *Geoffrey Jellineck: Jellineck. Geoffrey Jellineck. I'm the new art teacher.*
> *Chuck Noblet: Oh of course you are! Hi, I'm Chuck Noblet. Social Studies, creative writing, school newspaper, assistant to the principal …*
> *Geoffrey Jellineck: What don't you do!*
> *Chuck Noblet: Get my lesson plans in on time!*[22]

Strangers with Candy aired on Comedy Central in 1999 and 2000. Although it did not receive great reviews, it attracted a dedicated fan base. Colbert, working with Sedaris and Dinello, later resurrected *Strangers with Candy* for a full-length film adaptation, which premiered at the Sundance Film Festival in 2005.

Though his many comedic writing and acting jobs had not yet led to long-term work, Colbert was perfecting his humor, improvisational skills, and character-driven comedy. He was poised for the next phase of his career—the one that would make him well-known to audiences. Smithberg, the producer who had seen Colbert's *Good Morning America* work, hired Colbert as a writer for *The Daily Show* in 1997. At the time, Colbert thought it would be much the same type of writing he did at *Good Morning America*, and he did not see much future in the opportunity. Ironically, it would become one of the most important jobs of his career.

A New
Kind of Comedy

The Comedy Central television series *The Daily Show* hired Stephen Colbert as a writer and performer in 1997. As part of the ensemble cast, he would perfect a fake newsman persona and build partnerships with other comedians and writers. These partnerships led his career in a new direction. *The Daily Show* took Colbert from doubting his career choice and worrying about how he would support his family to earning awards, fame, and the respect of his peers.

Special Correspondent

The Daily Show is a late-night satirical news program that airs on Comedy Central. When the show premiered in 1996, it was hosted by former sports commentator Craig Kilborn. Comedian Jon Stewart took over as host in January 1999 and stayed with the show until 2015. Initially, Colbert was not impressed with the new opportunity. He thought the show relied too much on small, unrelated skits to get laughs. He also did not like the infighting among the show's producers. In short, he said, "I did not believe in the show, I did not watch the show, and they paid dirt. It was literally just sort of—it

Jon Stewart took *The Daily Show* in a more political direction.

was just a paycheck to show up."[23]

With Stewart as host, the show, which originally focused on pop culture, took on a political tone, satirizing news stories, political leaders, and, most pointedly, media coverage of news and current events. The format of the show was consistent: Stewart opened with a monologue that offered a satirical take on the day's news stories and issues. Next was a segment that featured an exchange with a "correspondent," played by one of several comedians who impersonated television news reporters and analysts. The correspondents generally sat at Stewart's anchor desk or pretended to report from another location, generally a live shot filmed in front of a green screen. The correspondents, often credentialed as some sort of "senior specialist," presented ridiculous or exaggerated takes on current events while Stewart asked a host of probing questions.

Faux News Correspondent

Colbert wrote material for *The Daily Show* and also played a news correspondent. While Stewart hosted *The Daily Show* as himself, Colbert, like the other correspondents, worked in character. Colbert developed a right-wing political pundit character that mocked the vanity of self-obsessed political correspondents. Colbert modeled himself after many media personalities but was particularly inspired by Stone Phillips, an anchorman who hosted *Dateline NBC*, and news anchor Geraldo Rivera, who is best known for his flamboyant style. Of his models for his correspondent role, Colbert has said,

> *My natural inclination was Stone Phillips, who has the greatest neck in journalism. And he's got the most amazingly severe head tilt at the end of tragic statements … and then I also used Geraldo Rivera, because he's got this great sense of mission. He just thinks he's gonna change the world with this report. He's got that early-'70s hip trench coat "busting this thing wide open" look going on.*[24]

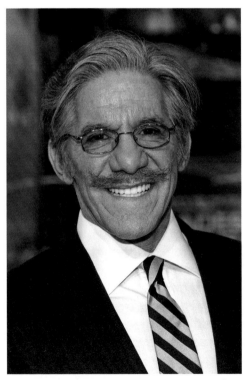

Geraldo Rivera was an inspiration for Colbert's character.

As Colbert developed the character, he also added the attributes of right-wing cable news pundit Bill O'Reilly, who hosted *The O'Reilly Factor* on

Oh Really, O'Reilly

Colbert used news personality Bill O'Reilly as a model for his character on *The Colbert Report*. O'Reilly is a bestselling author, syndicated columnist, and was the host of the political commentary program *The O'Reilly Factor* on Fox News Channel. After its debut in 1996, *The O'Reilly Factor* gained a wide following and was one of the highest-rated cable news shows on American television. The show was renamed *The Factor* after O'Reilly was fired in 2017. O'Reilly was one of the most powerful conservative forces in the media, although he claims he does not embrace a strict conservative ideology and is registered to vote as an independent.

Famous for his contentious style, O'Reilly brashly confronted those who opposed him. In one notorious encounter, O'Reilly shouted down Al Franken, who had written a book claiming that O'Reilly had misrepresented himself on numerous occasions. During the encounter, O'Reilly told Franken to "shut up," an exchange that was widely publicized. O'Reilly also engaged in heated arguments regarding what he called a "culture war" between those who embrace traditional values and

Fox News Network. Colbert also parodied Glenn Beck, Sean Hannity, and other right-wing conservative personalities. These real-life news stars were known for taking events and editorializing them, generally bringing a "fear factor" to the news in which they told their audience why they should be afraid of what is going on in the world, using their own interpretations of news events.

This sowing of fear and the air of self-importance and infallibility of many of these commentators were the key features of Colbert's invented persona. Colbert's

those wanting to change America. The strong opinions expressed by O'Reilly and other conservative pundits provided much of the material for *The Colbert Report*, described by Colbert as "personality driven news ... It's what [the host] thinks about the story as much as the story itself."[1]

1. Quoted in David Cote, "Joyce Words," *Time Out New York*, December 16, 2010. www.timeout.com/newyork/film/joycewords.

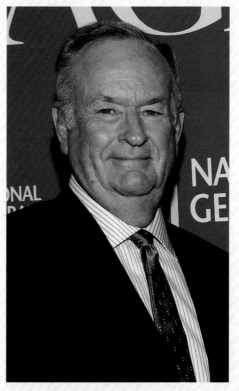

Bill O'Reilly greatly influenced Colbert as he developed his fake newsman persona.

character harkened back to earlier roles in which he enjoyed playing characters who were able to say absurd things. He often used this same technique when interviewing real experts for his otherwise fake news reports. Colbert said of this character, "On *The Daily Show*, I'm essentially a very high status character, but my weakness is that I'm stupid."[25]

He would also sometimes come out of nowhere with comments that flustered and flabbergasted his interviewee. Colbert said,

I'll go into an interview with a guy who runs a Beatles museum for instance, for The Daily Show, *and I'll confess to him that I don't know who* The Beatles *are. Like, I mean, obviously I know who they are, I just don't know—like, "What was their big hit? I know obviously they had more than one big hit, but what was that big one? The one they always whistled?" I don't mind seeming like a fool.*[26]

Bringing Out the Fool

Colbert was one of four fake correspondents who filmed segments for *The Daily Show* in the studio or from remote locations. He would frequently travel to different venues to file absurdly exaggerated reports on current news stories and conduct interviews with people related to the issue at hand. While the topics varied widely according to what news was making headlines, these reports typically poked as much fun at those who cover the news as at the news itself, even criticizing the entire genre of television news. Whatever the issue, Colbert's character spouted absurdities with what has now become his trademark serious expression and self-important smirk.

Colbert has described one of his favorite fake reporter segments and how it exposed the absurdity of broadcast news journalism. In a piece called "Death and Taxes," Colbert went to Saratoga Springs, New York, where a computer glitch had caused an X to be placed in the wrong box on all the county employees' annual tax forms. All the tax forms were printed with the X mark indicating that the 350 employees were deceased. Colbert covered the story in a unique way:

We went up there and covered it as if there had been a disaster where three hundred people had died … The reporter gets there and it is not what he thought it was but he won't let it go, especially that the people there are filled with rage, and I actually eventually got people to say that they were sad and that they were filled with rage. And it was a great triumph for me as a fake reporter to get them to buy into my idiocy.[27]

The Colbert character willingly humiliated himself for a laugh. Often, this meant taking a legitimate social issue, such as discrimination, to absurd extremes. For example, in one clip, Colbert satirized bigotry and discrimination when he interviewed people who said they were discriminated against because of the colors of their tattooed skin, saying they were forced to live separate but unequal lives reminiscent of African Americans during the civil rights era. As part of the segment, Colbert interviewed an African American man behind a civil ordinance banning tattoo parlors near public schools or churches. In his usual unflappable style, Colbert audaciously implied that the African American man was discriminating against people who have chosen to tattoo their skin.

In another clip, Colbert questioned a smoker who said she suffered discrimination similar to Rosa Parks. Colbert, in characteristic deadpan, ended the clip with a parody of the "I Have a Dream" speech given by civil rights leader Martin Luther King Jr. In the parody, Colbert proclaimed he had a dream that "one day we will all be judged by the content of our character and not the color of our lungs."[28]

Colbert's deadpan demeanor was sometimes enough to allow the joke to evolve on its own. In one episode, a rancher in Washington was told he could not develop his property because it was home to many endangered species, including Bigfoot. While the rancher, Jim Baum, railed at the absurdity of putting the mythical Bigfoot on the list, Colbert's interview with a Bigfoot expert topped the gag. The expert likewise said that it was absurd to put Bigfoot on the list, not because the creature was mythical, but because Bigfoot was alive and well, and not endangered.

The Daily Show's humor worked, in large part, because it so clearly echoed what goes on in real TV news shows. Many news shows are more about news anchors' personalities than the news. Often, news stories are inflated or trivialized by correspondents who do not always have a good grasp of the subject. Although everything seemed to be material for Stewart and his colleagues' mockery, *The Daily Show* did self-censor. When asked in an interview if there were any topics that were off limits on *The Daily Show*, Colbert replied,

> *Well, obviously real tragedy, like the [July 7, 2005] London bombing, is off limits. No one wants to do comedy about that. But I would say there's almost nothing that can't be mocked on a certain level as long as it doesn't involve loss of life or deep human tragedy. I don't think we ever looked at something and said that's too ridiculous to make more ridiculous. Contrary to what people may say, there's no upper limit to stupidity. We can make everything stupider.*[29]

Colbert and Stewart cohosted "Indecision 2008" for Comedy Central during the 2008 presidential election.

Faith and Following

Colbert is a devoted Catholic. Although he does not always follow strict religious doctrine, his faith is a very important part of his life:

I am highly variable in my devotion. From a doctrinal point of view or a dogmatic point of view or a strictly Catholic adherent point of view, I'm first to say that I talk a good game, but I don't know how good I am about it in practice. I saw how my mother's faith was very valuable to her and valuable to my brothers and sisters, and I'm moved by the words of Christ, and I'll leave it at that.[1]

Although Colbert does not divulge many details about his personal life, including those that pertain to his faith, he does attend church regularly and even teaches Sunday school. About working with his young students who do not know he is a comedic television star, Colbert said, "I get to actually talk to someone who will take me seriously when I talk about religion— albeit I have to find somebody who's seven to take me seriously."[2]

1. Quoted in Neil Strauss, "Stephen Colbert on Deconstructing the Colbert Nation," *Rolling Stone*, September 2, 2009. www.rollingstone.com/culture/news/stephen-colbert-on-deconstructing-the-news-religion-and-the-colbert-nation-20090902.

2. Quoted in Steven Daly, "The Second Most Powerful Idiot in America," *Telegraph*, May 18, 2008. www.telegraph.co.uk/culture/tvandradio/3673509/Stephen-Colbert-the-secondmost-powerful-idiot-in-America.html.

Colbert's time at *The Daily Show* helped him gain a deeper respect for the genre of political satire. He recalls that although he was not particularly political before joining *The Daily Show*, eventually Stewart "infected me with his spirit of satire … I learned to talk passionately about things you care about and be fair to a position that you don't agree with. I realized that I had stumbled into a perfect job for me."[30]

Showing His Wit

Colbert's correspondent performance was only part of what he contributed to *The Daily Show*. He also wrote a lot of the show's other content. In fact, Colbert and his fellow writers won three Emmys for Outstanding Writing for a Variety, Music or Comedy Program for *The Daily Show* in 2004, 2005, and 2006. Colbert recounts this as an especially good time for him. He loved writing stories through the lens of his newsman character and coming up with specific stories that lent themselves to spoofing. The format—a nightly, topical show driven by the day's headlines—demanded a lot of material to be produced quickly. This allowed Colbert to become less attached to his material. As he explained, "It [the show] has to be written by three, and the story just broke this morning."[31]

A Running Joke

Colbert was able to continue his collaboration with Steve Carell, who was also a correspondent on *The Daily Show*. Colbert and Carell performed a segment called "Even Stevphen," a mock debate that examined political and cultural events. The segment's name was a composite of the comedians' first names, Stephen and Steven, but also emphasized the similarities between the two. The duo would take on an issue to debate but generally ended up unleashing a chain of insults at one another, which often resulted in one or the other breaking down in tears. In an episode that aired in October 2000, for example, the senior pundit team poked fun at certain Halloween rituals. In one exchange, Carell taught Colbert how to trick-or-treat as Colbert staged a mock breakdown because he was not allowed this rite of passage as a child.

In another episode, Carell and Colbert debated Islam versus Christianity, and both comedians come off as the zealots that they are satirizing. To settle their debate about which religion is the one true religion, the two challenged each other to a "pray-off" to see who would be struck down first—Carell as he prayed to Allah or Colbert as he prayed to the Christian God. During this, Jon Stewart (who is Jewish) interrupted them to say that the skit was going on too long. At the end, they concluded that the two religions may not be so different after all.

Colbert's other important recurring segment on *The Daily Show* was "This Week in God," which featured Colbert's humorous take on religious topics in the news. In this skit, a "God Machine," a large black post with a red button, generated topics for discussion that ranged from the lighthearted to the subversively provocative. By pushing the button, Colbert would activate the God Machine, which would then flash religious imagery while making a "beep-boop-boop" sound (a recording of Colbert's voice). The flashing imagery would eventually slow down and land on a particular image that represented the topic to be examined in the segment. Colbert's "This Week in God," segment, which he performed from 2003 to 2005, won him a wide following and made the "God Machine" famous as an icon for the comedic—and often irreverent—examination of religious issues.

It All Happened One Election Night

The Daily Show's coverage of national and global political events and issues, though exaggerated for comical effect, generally had a serious point to make: exposing the flawed or illogical arguments of politicians or the weaknesses in media reporting. Notable segment topics included former president George W. Bush's war on terror and the occupation of Iraq.

It was the 2000 and 2004 presidential election campaigns, however, that rocketed the show's ratings—and Colbert's popularity—upward. In July 2000, Colbert and other cast members traveled to Philadelphia, Pennsylvania, to file reports from the floor of the Republican National Convention as part of the show's award-winning "Indecision 2000" coverage. Two weeks later, the show headed to Los Angeles, California, for the Democratic National Convention. The show used the ongoing headline "Indecision 2004" in its coverage of the election four years later, too.

In 2004, correspondents on *The Daily Show with Jon Stewart* began their coverage of election night with a song.

Covering a convention by poking fun at it seemed to appeal to many Americans, who, in many cases, tuned in to *The Daily Show* instead of watching the real news shows. Colbert described why political conventions are good material for comedy: "They're sales rallies where politicians say things people have already heard to people who already believe them."[32]

The effect of *The Daily Show* on the public is debated. Some complain it misinforms viewers because many tune in for the jokes and satire instead of reading or listening to real news. Others argue *The Daily Show* is actually an important source of news. A 2007 study by the Pew Research Center, for example, found *Daily Show* viewers to be more informed than audiences of news shows on Fox, CNN, or National Public Radio (NPR). The Pew Research Center determi ned that 54 percent of *Daily Show* viewers had a high level of knowledge about current events and political subjects—the highest score recorded.

Colbert does not believe that *The Daily Show*, nor his involvement in it, amounted to this kind of knowledge. He thinks the audience was already informed about world events, which was why they found the show's material funny: "I think you have to have some handle on what's happening in the world to get our jokes."[33]

Colbert went even further and said that though he sometimes wishes he could influence people's political philosophies, he does not believe he can or does. What he does is pure entertainment. Colbert thinks that since most news shows are built on stories that enhance people's fear and apprehension, shows such as *The Daily Show* are watched as an antidote to the real news: "I wish we had an effect on the way people think about politics, but I don't think we do. I see the show as a relief from the political process, especially now, when so much of politics is built on the idea of fear. We're falling down and going boom on camera."[34]

A Show of His Own

Since its debut, *The Daily Show* has launched many of its correspondents into independent careers. As Ben Karlin, the executive producer of the show, once said, "We don't have illusions about this show being the final stop for anyone. This is a training ground."[35] Early on, Colbert and Steve Carell were identified as talented comedians with serious breakout potential. When Steve Carell started getting offers from other networks, he left Comedy Central, going on to star on NBC's hit comedy series *The Office*.

Colbert also needed a new opportunity. After six years perfecting his character on *The Daily Show*, Colbert, along with Stewart and Karlin, conceived the idea of creating a spin-off of *The Daily Show*. As Stewart said, "Stephen has such encyclopedic knowledge and I figured using himself as the foundation of a character like that, there was no question he could do this every day. He was just ready."[36] The trio reportedly referred to the new show as their version of the conservative news show *The O'Reilly Factor* with Stephen Colbert. Comedy Central—not wanting to lose Colbert to another network—bought the idea and agreed to run *The Colbert Report* for eight episodes in 2005. It would go on to become one of Comedy Central's highest rated series, and Colbert would become a force in his own right.

The Importance
of Truthiness

After many years perfecting his fake reporter persona, Stephen Colbert took the leap to becoming his own boss. As a Second City troupe member and as an actor and writer on *The Daily Show*, Colbert had always been part of an ensemble. However, his new show, *The Colbert Report*, which launched on October 17, 2005, featured just him. Having his own show meant more responsibility for Colbert. He was fully in charge of all the show's material, and he was its sole star. *The Colbert Report* gave him more freedom with his comedy.

Leading for Laughs

In interviews before the show aired, critics asked Colbert whether he thought the American public would be interested in a show devoted entirely to his *Daily Show* character. On *The Daily Show*, Colbert's character was entertaining but clearly a secondary, supporting figure—just one of several people who made the show work. Whether Colbert could sustain a show on his own—or become a star in his own right—was unproven.

However, questions about the show's success were quickly answered the first week it aired, when 1 million viewers tuned in. Years later, the show continued to draw large audiences.

Designing Every Touch

The Colbert Report was produced in a studio in New York City. The set, called the "Eagle's Nest," was reminiscent of the set for The O'Reilly Factor. A series of LED displays featured patriotic images, such as the Stars and Stripes and the Statue of Liberty. Colbert described how the set was designed to amplify his status as host:

Everything on the show has my name on it, every bit of the set. One of the things I said to the set designer ... was "One of your inspirations should be [DaVinci's painting] The Last Supper. All the architecture of that room points at Jesus' head, the entire room is a halo, and he doesn't have a halo." And I said, "On the set, I'd like the lines of the set to converge on my head." And so if you look at the design, it all does, it all points at my head. And even radial lines on the floor, and on my podium, and watermarks in the

According to a 2014 Pew Research Center report, The Colbert Report became a particularly trusted source of political news for young men ages 18 to 29.

While The Daily Show is news parody, The Colbert Report was more about the cult of personality that characterizes many political opinion shows—making it the perfect vehicle for Colbert's deadpan humor and sharp commentary. Colbert's show focused more on the news correspondent inserting himself into the news—what he thinks about it, why his opinion is important—and trumping up himself as a character, in much the same way radio host Rush Limbaugh or news commentator Bill O'Reilly approached their shows. Colbert's character made fun of these news hosts' egotism. Columnist Johnny Frohlichstein summed up the difference between The Daily Show and The Colbert Report:

The main difference between these partners in comedy is the

images behind me, and all the vertices, are right behind my head. So there's a sort of sun-god burst quality about the set around me. And I love that. That's status.

We just try everything we can to pump up my status on the show.[1]

Colbert was the star of *The Colbert Report*, and he made sure his set design would not let viewers forget it.

1. Quoted in Nathan Rabin, "Interview: Stephen Colbert," A.V. Club, January 25, 2006. www.avclub.com/articles/stephen-colbert,13970/.

essence of their shows. Stewart focuses more on day-to-day news while fusing outlandish comparisons with hard facts. However, The Colbert Report is a complete character satire that focuses on the particulars of Colbert's character, with the actual news coming second.[37]

Part of Colbert's new responsibility for carrying a show was working long hours. He created and performed four new half-hour shows a week, about nine months a year. Colbert took it one show at a time. He tried to make each show fresh, without letting the following shows and the work involved in producing week by week influence the show he was currently working on. About the grueling demands of the job, Colbert remarked, "Early in this process I started calling this place 'the joy machine.' Because if it's not a joy machine, it's just a machine ... and then you get caught in the gears."[38] His work paid off. Colbert

The U.S. speed skating team is shown here posing in front of a Colbert Nation sign in 2009.

developed a loyal following, which he nicknamed the "Colbert Nation," and his Nation gave back to him in many ways.

Thinly Veiled Truth

Colbert imitated real-life news personalities to define and enhance his character's development. Some critics note that the most recognizable show Colbert parodied was Bill O'Reilly's nightly news show *The O'Reilly Factor*. In a review in the *New Yorker*, Nancy Franklin commented that Colbert "resembles nobody more than he does Bill O'Reilly, and like O'Reilly, he conveys fake humility and easy rage toward inappropriate targets."[39] O'Reilly has said he enjoyed the parody, finding Colbert's imitation not mocking but rather lighthearted and affectionate, even flattering. O'Reilly argued, "The formula of his program is, they watch the 'Factor' and they seize upon certain themes that work for him. He ought to be sending me a check every week, 'cause we're basically the research for his writers. I feel it's a compliment."[40]

However, Colbert said his show was far more than a simple parody of any single personality. He believes it targeted the current era in news coverage, in which the commentator had become the show. He sees this personality-driven aspect at work in many different arenas: "The show is not about O'Reilly. The show is about what is behind those things, which is: What I say is reality. And that never ends. Every politician is going to want to enforce that, or every person in Hollywood—every person."[41]

Colbert Changes Vocabulary

Colbert focused on how the media has changed from reporting noteworthy events to becoming more about the newsmakers. His act, which included inventing his own catchy witticisms and vocabulary, caught on with the media. For example, during *The Colbert Report's* first episode, Colbert coined the word "truthiness," which, with his character's typical anti-intellectual confidence, he defined as the truth one feels in the gut rather than what one can learn or know from books. As Colbert said during the episode,

> *Tonight's word: Truthiness. Now I'm sure some of the word-police, the wordinistas over at Websters, are gonna say, "Hey, that's not a word!" Well, anybody who knows me knows that I am no fan of dictionaries or reference books. They're elitist. Constantly telling us what is or isn't true, what did or didn't happen.*[42]

Colbert's truthiness highlights an increasingly real phenomenon in American culture, in which politicians and commentators claim that their own assertions, even when based on exaggeration or their own opinions, are more accurate than the truth. Language columnist Mark Peters has aptly defined truthiness as "the degraded condition of truth in media, government, nonfiction, and elsewhere."[43]

The word was inspired, in part, by former president George W. Bush's tendency to play loose and free with vocabulary when speaking in public. Colbert used Bush's 2005 nomination of lawyer Harriet Miers as Associate Justice of the U.S. Supreme Court in his explanation of "truthiness." At the time, many claimed that

Miers, a former White House counsel with close personal ties to Bush, was unqualified for such a high position, largely because she had never been a judge and lacked a clear record on many of the issues pertinent to the Supreme Court. However, as Colbert put it,

> We are divided between those who think with their head and those who know with their heart. Consider Harriet Miers. If you think about Harriet Miers, of course her nomination's absurd. But the president didn't say he thought about his selection … He didn't have to. He feels the truth about Harriet Miers. And what about Iraq? If you think about it, maybe there are a few missing pieces to the rationale for war, but doesn't taking Saddam out feel like the right thing?[44]

At the end of the first episode, Colbert further defined and defended his new concept in what would become his trademark deadpan mockery, claiming that while anyone could read the news, he was going to "feel" the news to the audience. Colbert later called this the "thesis statement" for the show, and truthiness has come to exemplify the way

In 2005, Colbert coined the term "truthiness" during the first episode of *The Colbert Report.*

American politicians redefine debates and the context of their comments. One year after the first episode aired, Colbert said,

> Language has always been important in politics, but language is incredibly important to the present political struggle … Because if you can establish an atmosphere in which information doesn't

mean anything, then there is no objective reality. The first show we did … was our thesis statement: What you wish to be true is all that matters, regardless of the facts.[45]

A Catchy Word

Truthiness continued to catch on in the news media and elsewhere. It still represents a powerful and important concept—and by some accounts, problem—facing society today. In January 2006, the American Dialect Society named "truthiness" the word of the year for 2005. Praise for the concept continued when Merriam-Webster, the American equivalent of the Oxford English Dictionary, announced "truthiness" as its word of the year for 2006. As Merriam-Webster president John Morse said about this honor, "We're at a point where what constitutes truth is a question on a lot of people's minds, and truth has become up for grabs. 'Truthiness' is a playful way for us to think about a very important issue."[46]

Indeed, Colbert used the concept of truthiness not only to mock but also to challenge Americans to think critically and examine reality, even as the media, the internet, and technology lulled them into doing otherwise. As critic Ethan Mills commented, "Through his brand of parody and satire, Stephen may be one of the greatest champions for the traditional values of truth and critical thinking on basic cable today. By relentlessly making fun of truthiness he can incite us to reflect on the direction of our culture, to question truthiness and those who wield it."[47]

In 2010, "truthiness" appeared in the New Oxford American Dictionary, with Colbert named as its founder. The word continues to spread and has even spawned the trend of adding "-iness" to the end of other words, such as describing misinformed people's ability to sound like they know what they are talking about as "referenciness." Stanford linguist Arnold Zwicky has gone so far as to call the suffix the "Colbert suffix."[48]

Colbert unveiled a new word during the 2016 presidential election campaign, in which Donald Trump and Hillary Clinton ran against each other. Colbert reminded his *Late Show* audience that 11 years prior, during the Bush administration, he had created the word "truthiness." He then revealed a new word in relation to Donald Trump—"Trumpiness." Colbert stated that Trumpiness does not have to involve truth, just feelings. With this, he not only brought the suffix back, but he also brought truthiness back into discussions.

Funny but True

Playing a character granted Colbert the freedom to say things that would unnerve viewers had they come out of the mouth of a real newscaster or even a sincere comedian. This is no accident: When Colbert, Stewart, and Karlin initially designed *The Colbert Report*, Colbert said he had to come off as sympathetic. Stewart seconded the notion, arguing that Colbert's character could pull off this naïveté nicely. Colbert said, "The audience wouldn't forgive Jon for saying things most comedians would want to say. But we can say almost anything, because it's coming out of the mouth of this character."[49]

Key to this accomplishment was the fact that Colbert never broke character—he played the smug, self-obsessed right-wing cable newscaster throughout each episode, no matter how outrageous his commentary. He generally made his point by saying the exact opposite, keeping a poker face all the while. In one episode, for example, Colbert did a sketch about eating disorders, looking directly into the camera and saying, "Girls, if we can't see your ribs, you're ugly."[50] The statement was over the top, yet still made a point about the pressure women are under to be thin. The connection between truth and over-the-top humor is what made *The Colbert Report* work.

No subject was safe. Another example of Colbert's starkly humorous takes included knowledge—"I don't trust books; they're all fact, no heart."[51]

The Nation Makes It Work

Colbert's humor also worked in part because of his relationship with his audience. Colbert commented that he considers his audience part of the show, so much so that his show had two characters—Colbert and the audience. "They're the other character," he said. "If they're not there, then I've got no friction. I've got no one to talk to."[52]

The audience not only got Colbert's desire to make them a part of the show, they actively sought out chances to prove it. Before each show, Colbert asked the audience to shout "Stephen" as loud as they could. The audience always kept it up until Colbert, in character, made them stop. People waited in long lines outside the show hoping for a chance to become part of the audience.

Wit Through Bullet Points

Like many real news shows, Colbert's show had a set format that was followed fairly religiously every night. After the show's opening sequence, *The Colbert Report* typically began with an imitation of a news broadcast that featured the week's events and top stories. A particular news item generally led into the show's signature segment: "The Wørd." In "The Wørd," Colbert spoke out on a particular topic while satirical bullet points flashed on a side screen. These bullet points often undercut, contradicted, or conveyed the true meaning of Colbert's statements in some way; sometimes they just mocked the host. In one segment, for example, Colbert said that Africa had more elephants than it did 10 years earlier. Colbert then said that he did not know whether it was a fact that elephants were making a comeback, and the screen flashed, "It isn't."[53] The segment is a parody of Bill O'Reilly's "Talking Points" segment, in which O'Reilly talks while captions that sum up the heart of his ideas appear on the screen.

On the January 29, 2007, episode of *The Colbert Report*, Colbert discussed Wikilobbying and Wikiality. He came up with the Wikilobbying term in a discussion of how Microsoft was paying people to edit their Wikipedia entries to make the company look more favorable. Colbert suggested that for Microsoft to be more trustworthy, they should pay people to write on their Wikipedia page that people were trusting the company again. In response, the screen flashed, "Reality has become a commodity."[54] The satire of the commentary was enhanced with these tidbits, allowing the skit to become a sight gag as well.

One of the most concrete ways Colbert became part of America's cultural landscape was through language. Many of the words he coined on *The Colbert Report* were picked up in the media and ended up entering the popular lexicon. While the most enduring may be "truthiness," there are a host of others.

Colbert used his wit to develop words and catchphrases that mocked larger trends in American society. For example, he developed the term "Wikiality" to mock America's tendency to rely on the editable online encyclopedia Wikipedia, where, as he put it, "any user can change any entry, and if enough users agree with them, it becomes true."[55] He introduced the term—a blend of "reality" and "Wiki"—during his July 31, 2006, "Wørd" segment, saying that "together we can create a reality that we all agree on—the reality we just agreed on."[56] Through Wikiality, Colbert brilliantly skewered the idea that the truth is whatever Wikipedia users say it is. "Wikiality is the idea that something becomes true if enough people say it," explained Ethan Mills in the book *Stephen Colbert and Philosophy*. "Stephen doesn't like being told that George Washington owned slaves, but through Wikiality it can become true that Washington was not a slave owner!"[57]

Colbert also coined the term "wordinista," which he defined disparagingly as anyone who sticks up for the proper use of the English language. Defending truthiness, Colbert declared, "What is it with you wordinistas telling me what is and isn't a word?"[58] As Jason Southworth, a philosophy instructor at Fort Hays State University in Kansas, described,

From the context, it is clear that one thing a wordinista does is tell people what is and is not a word. This isn't enough to capture the whole meaning of the term, however. The "What is it with you" prior to the term also implies that the word is meant to have a negative connotation ... The "inista" part of the word should make most people immediately think of the word "Sandinista" ... a radical Marxist political party from Nicaragua. So, it seems "wordinista" is also intended to suggest a radical disposition.

Putting these things together, a "wordinista" is a person who is radical about correcting others about their misuse of words and their use of non-established words.[59]

Colbert's language is popular but also telling. As Adam Sternbergh of *New York Magazine* said,

Colbertisms ring throughout the land—and not just from the mouth of Colbert. The best testament to the triumph of the Colbertocracy is that you can now hear a Colbert line like "I believe the government that governs best is the government that governs least, and by these standards, we have set up a fabulous government in Iraq" and devoid of context, you might genuinely wonder if it came from a parodist, a pundit, or from the president himself.[60]

Repeat Offenders

Another popular segment on *The Colbert Report* was "Better Know a District," in which Colbert interviewed a member of Congress who represented a particular district in the House of Representatives. Each interview was preceded by a humorous history lesson on the district. The interviews typically featured off-the-wall questions that sought to mock the representatives, catch them off guard, or otherwise insult or confuse them. For example, Colbert asked Virginia Congressman Bobby

When filming "Better Know a District" for *The Colbert Report* on May 18, 2007, Colbert asked Raul Grijalva, a Democratic representative for Arizona, if he had any superpowers.

Scott if he had any tattoos, and when he answered that he did not, Colbert asked him, "Would you think about getting an American flag tattoo to show your love for America?"[61] When Scott said no, Colbert asked him if he loved his country. In another memorable clip, Colbert revealed that Georgia Republican Lynn Westmoreland could not recite the Ten Commandments, even after the congressman spearheaded a campaign to have them displayed in both the House of Representatives and the Senate. The popularity of "Better Know a District" inspired a number of spin-offs, including "Better Know a Founder," "Better Know a Candidate," and "Better Know a President."

Colbert's New Words

Since introducing "truthiness" on *The Colbert Report*'s debut episode, Colbert has continued to come up with more new words, often by blending two or more unrelated words together. These words include Wikiality, Wikilobbying, Trumpiness, Lincolnish, superstantial, freem, and eneagled.

These words have become part of the language of Colbert's fans, and some, such as "truthiness," have become a part of culture in general. This shows that not only is Colbert important to his fans, but he is also an important part of pop culture.

Colbert used one "Better Know a Founder" skit to mock the reality fashion show *Project Runway* by gathering three Thomas Jefferson imitators in a competition he called "America's Top Jefferson." The skit opened with Tim Gunn, who has a prominent role on *Project Runway*, critiquing the three Jeffersons' costumes. Colbert next interviewed the three Jeffersons, asking them a variety of questions and keeping score. At the end of the contest, Colbert concluded, "And looking at the score card, I have not kept very good score, I have no idea who is in the lead."[62] Colbert ended the segment by tossing a coin to crown America's top Jefferson.

The Guests Keep Coming

No matter which segment was featured, the final third of *The Colbert Report* was almost always a guest interview. Colbert had no problem attracting guests from all walks of life. Just a few notables who have appeared on the show include former president Barack Obama, former NPR correspondent Eric Weiner, *New York Times* columnist Maureen Dowd, actress Jane Fonda, comedian Conan O'Brien, boxer Sugar Ray Leonard, comedian Steve Martin, artist William Wegman, former vice president Joe Biden, and former secretary of state Henry Kissinger.

Former president Barack Obama appeared on *The Colbert Report* three times.

Not surprisingly, most of the politicians, authors, and other celebrity guests got mildly ridiculed by Colbert. When he interviewed John Mica, Republican representative from Florida, for example, Colbert asked in a deep, serious voice whether Mica had to take off his toupee when he went through security. Most of Colbert's guests are in on the joke. As Steven Daly wrote,

> Colbert's character never bullies or shouts at his guests. "The emotion of the shouting would shut the guest down," [Colbert] observes. Perhaps it's this kinder, gentler approach that regularly leads to the remarkable sight of apparently sane guests getting

sucked into the parallel universe of Colbert's famous neologism "truthiness," that is feelings-as-logic. On The Colbert Report *one regularly sees real politicians getting so bamboozled that they can barely respond when Colbert blithely insists, "I'm not making this up—I'm imagining it!" Or when he bellows forth the victorious non-sequitur [a statement that does not relate to what was previously said], "I accept your apology!"*[63]

Colbert always said he did not ambush his guests: "Everybody knows what they're in for with me. I say exactly the same thing to everyone before the interview: 'I'm not an assassin. I do the show in character—and he's an idiot; he's willfully ignorant of everything we're going to talk about. Disabuse me of my ignorance. Don't let me put words in your mouth.'"[64]

Some of the interviews ended up making significant political points. In one segment, Colbert interviewed Daniel Ellsberg, who was responsible for leaking the Pentagon Papers to the mainstream media in 1971. At a time when the Vietnam War was becoming unpopular, the Pentagon Papers proved that the United States had illegally expanded the Vietnam War and that the government had deliberately misinformed the American people about various aspects of the war. At the time, Ellsberg was considered a traitor, and some even suggested he should be tried for treason. Ellsberg was the first man to be criminally prosecuted for a defense leak. Colbert used the interview to compare Ellsberg to Wikileaks founder Julian Assange, who in 2010 and 2011 leaked numerous secret government papers to the media. Through his interview with Ellsberg, Colbert was able to freely comment on the concept of free speech and how it is only through the passage of time that Ellsberg is now a revered public figure in the fight for the protection of leaks as a First Amendment right.

Although Colbert worked with a script—he wrote much of his own material for the show—he also improvised according to how his interviews played out. Indeed, ad-libbing much of the show was a chance to display his razor-sharp wit. Colbert's former college roommate Eric Goodman, who has worked for Disney, commented on Colbert's ability: "You wonder, 'How does

Stephen do it?' ... He has to twist it in his head so he says something completely absurd, which he would never say in real life, but seems completely plausible."[65]

Not Bringing the Character Home

Colbert so thoroughly immersed himself in his on-air persona that, not surprisingly, he had to make a conscious effort to abandon it when he entered his home life. He had to make sure to leave behind not just the stress of the job but also his character when he returned home to his family each night. In an interview with *Vanity Fair*, he explained,

> *Letting go and not being the boss is much harder [at the end of the day] than letting go of my character ...*
>
> *That's why I drive myself home at night ... The network would happily ... send me home in a car. But I'd work the entire way home, and I need more than the 30 seconds from the car to the front door to become a dad and a husband again. So I drive home and I crank my tunes. And by the time I get there, I'm normal again.*[66]

Many critics wondered if Colbert could go on to do important work outside his *Colbert Report* character. Out of character, Colbert became a vocal supporter of a number of causes and eventually translated his experience and comedic skills to new heights of television success.

Changing Politics and Giving Back

Stephen Colbert has had a unique cultural impact. He has used his fame to bring attention to important causes and has highlighted social and political problems by using humor and satire. By using the very forms of media he sometimes mocked on *The Colbert Report*, he has been able to get his message out quickly and in a contemporary manner, and his fans have responded.

The Presidential Comic

In April 2006, Colbert was asked to deliver the keynote speech at the annual White House Correspondents' Association dinner—an event that typically features a good-natured roast of the president. When Associated Press reporter Mark Smith booked Colbert for the event, he said he knew little of the satirist's act, except that "he not only skewers politicians, he skewers those of us in the media."[67]

After opening remarks, Colbert stepped to the podium. With then-president George W. Bush sitting just one seat away, Colbert mercilessly lampooned Bush's policies on the Iraq War and other events. Completely in his high-status idiot character, Colbert remarked with false admiration and a straight face, "He believes the same thing Wednesday that he believed on Monday, no matter what happened Tuesday. Events can change; this man's beliefs never will."[68] Colbert also mocked core Republican beliefs when he said, "I believe the government that governs best is the government that governs least. And by these standards, we have set up a fabulous government in Iraq."[69]

On April 29, 2006, Colbert gave the keynote speech at the White House Correspondents' Association dinner.

Not content to lampoon only the president and his party, Colbert delivered a scathing critique of Washington's press corps, the very people who invited him to the event. He accused them of simply buying into the administration's reasons for supporting tax cuts, using the supposed presence of weapons of mass destruction as a reason to invade Iraq, and minimizing global warming.

Many reviews of Colbert's performance at the 2006 White House Correspondents' Association dinner were highly critical. Several inferred that the comedian did not do well because he did not get many big laughs in the room. According to one reviewer, however, the reaction in the room no longer matters because Colbert's performance, like many important public events, was immediately posted on the internet. Colbert had chosen to play to his audience, not to the room, knowing they would see it later.

Interpreter for the Masses

Overall, Colbert's performance was much more pointed than other comics had been at previous dinners, and afterward, almost everyone in the media had an opinion of it. Richard Cohen of

The Part of a Patriot

While Colbert pokes fun at the reasons the U.S. military is in Iraq and elsewhere, he remains a dedicated advocate of soldiers. In June 2009, Colbert brought his show to Iraq and filmed a week's worth of episodes alongside U.S. troops stationed at Camp Victory in Baghdad. He humorously pointed out that many had been deployed to the beleaguered nation multiple times. "It must be nice here in Iraq because I understand some of you keep coming back again and again," he said. "You've earned so many frequent flyer miles, you've earned a free ticket to Afghanistan,"[1] where the United States had also been at war since 2001.

Wearing a suit and tie specially created for him in the army camouflage pattern, Colbert drew rousing applause when he showed a clip of himself going through a mock version of the Army's basic training regimen. The highlight of the series occurred when one of Colbert's guests, General Ray Odierno, the commander of U.S. forces in Iraq, received a prerecorded message from the White House in which President Barack Obama jokingly "ordered" the commander to give Colbert a military haircut. The general agreed, and Colbert's head was shaved to thunderous applause.

A year later, in September 2010, Colbert offered another salute to the troops when he devoted two more episodes to honoring American service members in a special called "Been There, Won That: The Returnification

the *Washington Post* called the comedian just plain rude. Chris Lehmann wrote in the *Observer* that "the material came off as shrill and airless."[70] Others, however, lauded the speech. Former *TIME* TV critic James Poniewozik wrote that Colbert's points,

of the American-Do Troopscape." As Colbert said, "No matter how you felt about this war, we Americans sent them off to fight it. And now that it's over, we should thank them. And quickly, because I think a lot of them are getting sent to Afghanistan."[2] The special episodes were filmed in the studio and featured a number of high-profile guests, including Vice President Joe Biden and General Odierno. The audience was filled with service members as well as active-duty members from Iraq and Afghanistan via satellite.

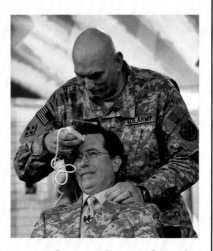

General Ray Odierno shaved Colbert's head in 2009 after receiving a message from President Obama to do so.

The Army honored Colbert in 2015 with its Outstanding Civilian Service Award. The third highest honor within the Department of the Army Civilian Awards, the honor represented his substantial contributions to the U.S. Army community.

1. Quoted in AP, "Stephen Colbert Shaves Head for US Troops in Iraq," CBSNews.com, June 8, 2009. www.cbsnews.com/news/stephen-colbert-shaves-head-for-us-troops-in-iraq/.

2. Quoted in Dave Itzkoff, "Colbert to Welcome Home Iraq Troops with Specials," New York Times, August 20, 2010. www.nytimes.com/2010/08/21/arts/television/21arts-COLBERT-TOWEL_BRF.html.

though sometimes cringe-inducing, were right on target. *New York Times* columnist Frank Rich agreed, calling the speech "the defining moment of the 2006 [midterm election] campaign."[71]

Colbert defended his appearance, saying he was there to tell jokes. He said his jokes were aimed not at the audience in the room, but rather at his television audience (the event was broadcast on C-SPAN). Indeed, Colbert was primarily playing to the millions of people who viewed the speech on the internet. Amid the media buzz about Colbert's performance, the video of his speech went viral. Within 2 days of the event, 2.7 million people watched it on YouTube alone. As *New York Magazine*'s editor Adam Sternbergh noted,

> [Colbert] was invited to give the keynote speech at a dinner for the president and wound up delivering a controversial, possibly very funny, possibly horribly unfunny, possibly bravely patriotic, and possibly near-seditious monologue that earned him a crazed mob of lunatic followers who await his every command.[72]

Colbert brought criticism of the president, as well as of the news media, directly to the public. He turned a relatively small, typically uncontroversial event into a national debate and invited the American public to participate. Colbert recognized that this was his target audience—and this tactic would be what would propel him to the forefront of political discourse. In this way, Colbert made the mainstream media irrelevant by going directly to the public. As Poniewozik wrote in *TIME*, Colbert merely pointed out "how authority is fragmented and democratized in the Internet era." While in decades past the job of the media was to "assess and interpret for the masses,"[73] the internet has made that function obsolete. Colbert and others like him realize that harnessing the internet means harnessing public opinion.

The Power of a Following

Colbert's accurate imitation of blustering news punditry and hilarious commentary had already earned him a fan base among viewers who appreciated parody and political satire. Following his razor-sharp press corps speech, however, Colbert's popularity reached new heights. The Colbert Nation became a force in itself.

Colbert encouraged his viewers not just to watch his show, but to become part of the joke and join in the game to influence the world. According to Colbert, he did not encourage his fans to behave as a bloc that supported the show. Though Colbert's character often prefaced his remarks by addressing his audience presumptuously as "Nation," the group of devoted fans and supporters known as the Colbert Nation evolved on its own. As Colbert put it in a 2009 interview with *Rolling Stone*, "We invented the Colbert Nation, but then we discovered it was real. We didn't make it happen, they self-organized it. I love that relationship. We can't always have it, and you can't force that. You just have to acknowledge it."[74]

The Colbert Nation enthusiastically adopted causes taken up by Colbert, in or out of character. These sometimes stunt-like acts typically landed him, his show, and his audience in the news. For example, Colbert once mentioned on the show that the Saginaw Spirit minor league hockey team was holding a name-our-mascot contest. Colbert asked his fans to bombard the team's website with votes for "Steagle Colbeagle the Eagle"—which subsequently won and became the team's secondary mascot for the 2006 to 2007 season.

Similarly, in 2006, Colbert urged his followers to vote in an online poll to name a Hungarian bridge that crosses the Danube River the "Stephen Colbert Bridge." The comedian received more than 6.3 million votes—millions more than any other entry. The ambassador to Hungary, however, declared that according to Hungarian law, Colbert was not qualified because he was not Hungarian and he was also still living.

In 2008, a spider was even named for Colbert—the *Aptostichus stephencolberti*—after biologist Jason Bond was watching an episode of *The Colbert Report* in which Colbert was wishing he had a spider named after him.

Fake Campaign, Real Politics

Colbert's infectious comedic personality and his ability to galvanize his fans prompted him to launch a fake run for the presidency. A fake campaign was the perfect platform to send out

Colbert Gives Back

Colbert is known for his charitable activities as well as his antics. He has raised many thousands of dollars for a variety of causes, including Autism Speaks, a national organization that researches causes of and cures for autism; the Yellow Ribbon Fund, which assists injured service members and their families; and the Canadian support group Parkinson Society. Like all things associated with Colbert, these fund-raising events generally feature plenty of good-natured comedy.

In April 2011, Colbert appeared on the comedy show *Late Night with Jimmy Fallon* to sing Rebecca Black's pop song "Friday." Colbert promised viewers that if they could raise $26,000 for Donors Choose, a charity that donates classroom supplies to underfunded schools, he would perform the song. "Friday," written and performed by Black, became a viral hit in 2011 with more than 82 million views of its music video online. At the same time, it gained much negative attention after it received more than 1.6 million "dislikes" from YouTube viewers. Colbert chose the song because he thought its popularity would make his parody of it instantly recognizable. The musical extravaganza featured cheerleaders and appearances by the musical group The Roots and *American Idol* contestant Taylor Hicks. A reviewer for *Rolling Stone* wrote, "There's a lot to love in this clip, but the best thing about it is that everyone involved is celebrating the year's most absurd pop hit rather than making fun of the 13-year-old Black."[1]

1. Matthew Perpetua, "Stephen Colbert and Jimmy Fallon Perform Rebecca Black's 'Friday,'" *Rolling Stone*, April 4, 2011. www.rollingstone.com/music/news/stephen-colbert-and-jimmy-fallon-perform-rebecca-blacks-friday-20110404.

his unflagging message—that American politics and politicians, as well as the news media's reporting of politics and politicians, border on a joke.

Colbert first hinted at a 2008 presidential run when he appeared on talk shows to promote his book *I Am America (And So Can You!)*. On Larry King's CNN talk show on October 14, 2007, for example, Colbert put forth the absurd proposition that he might possibly seek the nomination from both the Republican and Democratic parties, arguing that this demonstrated true courage because he could lose twice.

Colbert is shown here with a copy of his book *I Am America (And So Can You!)* at a New York City book signing on October 24, 2007.

Before Colbert officially announced his candidacy, he also spoke to supporters as a guest contributor in Maureen Dowd's October 14 *New York Times* column, poking fun at the fact that most presidential candidates tend to be white, Christian males: "I know why you want me to run, and I hear your clamor. It's clear that the voters are desperate for a white, male, middle-aged Jesus-trumpeting alternative."[75]

On October 16, 2007, Colbert officially announced his campaign to run for president in South Carolina, his home state. With red, white, and blue balloons floating down on the set of his own show, Colbert proclaimed, "After nearly 15 minutes of soul searching, I have heard the call. Nation, I will seek the office of the president of the United States. I am doing it!"[76]

Leading the Party

As the media picked up the story, Colbert's poll numbers began to actually climb, even beating some of his contenders: A Public Opinion Strategies national poll found that Colbert was drawing 2.3 percent of the support in the Democratic race, putting him ahead of serious candidates Bill Richardson and Dennis Kucinich, both at 2.1 percent, and putting him only slightly behind the future vice president, Joe Biden, who was drawing 2.7 percent. Momentum continued to build, and by the next week, a Rasmussen poll showed that in a three-way race against Democrat Hillary Clinton and Republican Rudy Giuliani, the TV personality was drawing a remarkable 13 percent—far higher than most third-party candidates in previous presidential elections.

In fact, Colbert was doing so well in the polls that some people did not appreciate the joke. Many argued that in using the presidential election to spread a comedic message, Colbert had crossed a line. A spokesman for Richardson, for example, said, "This is a serious election with serious consequences and we are not going to comment on this ridiculous exercise."[77] The Colbert Nation, on the other hand, was wildly supportive. Almost immediately, Colbert became an internet sensation. A Facebook group called "1,000,000 Strong for Stephen T. Colbert" garnered more than 850,000 members within a week of his announcement.

However, the run was not to be. After learning that it cost $35,000 to be included in the Republican primary in South Carolina, Colbert dropped his plans to run as a Republican. He did pay $2,500 to run as a Democrat, but in the end, the South Carolina Democratic Party dropped him from the ballot. He acknowledged that the rejection stung, even though he joked until the very end: "They tell you when you're a child that anyone can run for President. But apparently not you, Stephen Colbert."[78]

Though Colbert was never serious about actually running for the presidency, the real support he garnered for his fake candidacy seemed to reflect the perception that politics has degenerated into a form of entertainment. Again and again, his comedy shows a serious side that resonates with many mainstream Americans.

Balancing Jon Stewart's Reasonableness

In October 2010, Colbert further blurred the line between entertainment and politics, this time teaming up with Jon Stewart to satirize the way in which political speech in America has increasingly taken a hostile, paranoid, and exaggerated tone. The pair staged a protest in Washington, D.C., called the "Rally to Restore Sanity and/or Fear." It was intended to satirize other such events, such as the "Restoring Honor" rally held two months earlier by right-wing advocate Glenn Beck, which had a strong religious focus and a conservative political agenda.

In contrast, the Rally to Restore Sanity and/or Fear was a plea for sanity and civility in political discourse. Part comedy festival, part concert, and part parody of media-hyped political rallies, Stewart described the rally as a place for people who "think shouting is annoying, counterproductive, and terrible for your throat; who feel that the loudest voices shouldn't be the only ones that get heard; and who believe that the only time it's appropriate to draw a Hitler mustache on someone is when that person is actually Hitler"[79] to join them in an effort to tone down the national dialogue on political and social issues. The event provided a perfect vehicle for the two comedians to lampoon American political divisions and

Tens of thousands of people attended the Rally to Restore Sanity and/or Fear on October 30, 2010. The protest was organized by Colbert and Stewart, shown here in patriotic attire.

the media's role in polarizing debates. It touched on many of the themes satirized by Colbert's on-air persona—fear mongering, partisan punditry, and sensationalism.

Interestingly, Colbert's part of the rally was originally slated to be called the "Rally to Restore Truthiness." In an interview shortly before the event, Colbert commented on the decision to keep the march primarily about fear:

> I don't think we actually need to restore [truthiness]. I think it is
> perfectly healthy. I think if you just look around you, I doubt that
> many people in American politics are acting on facts. Everybody
> on both sides is acting on the things that move them emotionally
> the most. And that is the most successful way to behave. By keep-
> ing fear alive, we are keeping truthiness alive at the same time.
> Action out of emotion is all that truthiness is about—making your
> decisions based upon how you feel. Right now, it seems like fear
> is the strongest emotion that motivates us.[80]

The Rally to Restore Sanity was first announced on *The Daily Show* on September 16, 2010, when Stewart declared his intention to "take it down a notch for America."[81] The same night, Colbert declared on his show his intention to have a "March to Keep Fear Alive" by saying, "I am sorry, Jon Stewart, I will not take it down a notch, I will notch it up a skosh."[82] Colbert mockingly stated that he would participate in the rally only to uphold truthiness and fight Stewart's unnerving reasonableness.

The rally immediately gained support on the internet, with more than a quarter million people announcing they would attend. Those who could not make the trip to Washington, D.C., were offered satellite rallies in other major cities, including Chicago, Los Angeles, and Honolulu, Hawai'i. Originally scheduled to take place in the area by the Washington Monument, the turnout grew so large that the event was relocated to the east end of the National Mall, facing the Capitol. One estimate put the actual crowd at around 215,000. In addition, the rally was broadcast live on Comedy Central and C-SPAN. The Comedy Central broadcast alone drew an estimated 2 million viewers. An additional 570,000 viewers watched the live video stream of the event online.

Taking Comedy Seriously

Many of the people attending the rally carried signs or wore costumes that expressed ironic political messages or pleas for more civil discourse. One group of people dressed as tea bags mocked the Tea Party, a conservative movement known for its anti-immigration, antigovernment stance and support of what the Tea Party defines as traditional American values. Other rally attendees simply held signs to satirize American political views. Some featured slogans such as "It's a sad day when our politicians are comical and I have to take our comedians seriously." Other signs said things such as "Facts are like opinions, except they're true," and "My opinions change with new information."[83]

Comedy sketches were woven throughout the program, and celebrities such as John Legend, Sheryl Crow, Kid Rock, Star Wars droid R2-D2, and Ozzy Osbourne also joined the fun.

Since Colbert spoke only through his character, it was up to Stewart to make the serious closing remarks, which summarized the overriding theme of the rally—politicians are overly partisan, and the sensationalist media hypes and even creates issues for Americans to fear and fight about:

Many people who attended the Rally to Restore Sanity and/or Fear carried signs poking fun at American politics.

The country's twenty-four hour politico, pundit, perpetual panic conflictinator did not cause our problems. But its existence makes solving them that much harder.

The press can hold its magnifying glass up to our own problems, bringing them into focus ... or they can use that magnifying glass to light ants on fire and then perhaps host a week of shows on the sudden, unexpected, dangerous flaming ant epidemic.[84]

Stewart was so moved by the turnout that he claimed, "Sanity will always be and has always been in the eye of the beholder; and to see you here today and the kind of people that you are, has restored mine."[85] Stewart and Colbert's joint venture gave voice to Americans fed up with current media and political tactics. As for Colbert, his persona had clearly become a national phenomenon that continued to gain support and become a force in and of itself.

His Part on the Hill

Colbert did not just make fun of politics and politicians—he also brought serious issues to the forefront. For example, in 2010, he took on the issue of migrant labor and sought to raise awareness of the plight of migrant workers. Many such people work temporarily in the United States. They harvest crops during long hours in the hot sun, and many live in unsanitary work camps. Colbert became intrigued by a campaign sponsored by the United Farm Workers of America, which was fighting to give undocumented immigrants a way to gain citizenship. The campaign, called "Take Our Jobs," gave Americans an opportunity to work the many agricultural jobs typically done by migrant workers. The point of the program was to show Americans how difficult, labor-intensive, and poorly paid agricultural jobs are and to show that they do not in fact threaten American jobs, as is frequently charged.

Colbert spent a day on a farm in upstate New York crating corn and picking beans. Shortly after, in September 2010, Colbert testified before Congress on behalf of the United Farm Workers. He told the packed hearing room on Capitol Hill, "I like talking about people who don't have any power … and it seems like some of the least powerful people in the United States are migrant workers who come and do our work but don't have any rights as a result." Describing his work in the fields as very hard, Colbert went on to jokingly say, "This brief experience made me realize why so few Americans are clamoring to begin an exciting career as a migrant farm worker."[86]

In September 2010, Colbert testified—in character—during the "Protecting America's Harvest" hearing.

While some commentators thought that Colbert had gone too far by testifying before Congress in character, others felt Colbert did exactly what he meant to do—bring attention to an important issue. As journalist Peter Grier put it,

Never underestimate the power of pure attention. Hundreds of thousands (maybe millions) of Americans tomorrow will know more about the conditions in which migrants work because a comedian picked corn for a day. It doesn't matter that Colbert did not have a three-point plan for passing a bill that allows illegal migrant workers to work towards legal status by remaining in agricultural jobs. Today those workers are less faceless than they were before.[87]

By poking fun at the powers-that-be, Colbert harnesses enthusiasm for the issues he thinks are important. In the process, he leaves his wide audience better informed.

A Leader
in Late Night

The joy machine had finally become just a machine for Stephen Colbert by 2015. He was ready to leave his old persona behind and return to himself. After the end of *The Colbert Report*, Colbert took over one of the most popular late-night shows. CBS's *The Late Show* had been hosted by David Letterman since its debut in 1993. With Letterman retiring, CBS asked Colbert to be the host, but not in his *Colbert Report* persona. He would host as himself. On Tuesday, September 8, 2015, Colbert officially took over *The Late Show* and brought his comedy and truthiness to a different stage.

The Colbert Show's *Final Bow*

In early 2014, Colbert announced the end of his comedic news persona. The successful *Colbert Report* would end because the joy was leaving the show. As Colbert's persona grew, the comedy began to take a sharper edge. Colbert knew it was time to stop before the joke was over. "It wasn't because I didn't like it anymore—I still liked it—but I just thought, *I'm not sure if I can actually keep this up without hurting someone.*"[88]

One week after the announcement, everyone knew where Colbert was headed next: late-night network television. Before he had announced the end of *The Colbert Report*, Colbert had been offered an opportunity. In early April 2014, David Letterman, the host of *The Late Show* on CBS, announced his retirement. CBS approached Colbert and asked if he wanted to take Letterman's place. On April 10, 2014, CBS announced that Colbert would be replacing Letterman on *The Late Show*.

On December 18, 2014, the last episode of *The Colbert Report* aired on Comedy Central. Interviewers and the Colbert Nation asked if the old persona would make an appearance in the future:

He's out there like King Arthur, if anyone needs him to come back to be wrong about something on a professional level. Because he's professionally wrong about things. But I think I have an intimate enough relationship with the audience that they don't want him between us. Do you know what I mean? The last time I did it, they enjoyed it, but I think they enjoyed me just being me more—and so do I. That's why I took this gig.[89]

Colbert is shown here during the break between his two shows.

Colbert's Other Work

Colbert has lent his talents to many other projects. In 2003, he coauthored the satirical novel *Wigfield: The Can-Do Town That Just May Not* and performed in a stage adaptation of the novel the same year. Other acting credits include a small supporting role in the 2005 film adaptation of *Bewitched* and a role in the film adaptation of *Strangers with Candy* the same year. In November 2008, his Christmas special *A Colbert Christmas: The Greatest Gift of All!* aired on Comedy Central. In 2011, Colbert had a costarring role in Stephen Sondheim's *Company* revival on Broadway.

Over the years, Colbert has made guest appearances on several television series, including *Law & Order: Criminal Intent*, *The Office*, *The Mindy Project*, and the improvisational comedy show *Whose Line Is It Anyway?* He has also voiced characters for several popular animated shows and movies including *The Simpsons*, *American Dad*, *Mr. Peabody & Sherman*, *Monsters vs. Aliens*, *BoJack Horseman*, and *Rick and Morty*.

In 2017, Colbert came back to his roots, guest staring on his former *Strangers with Candy* coworkers' new

During the break between his last episode on Comedy Central and his new job at CBS, Colbert grew a thick beard and gave it a funny name: a Colbeard. For Colbert, growing a beard was perfect for the break between shows. "I have not allowed this to happen to my face since college because I've been working professionally pretty constantly since then," he said. However, there was more to the beard. "It turns out the real Stephen Colbert had a beard the whole time, I was just so deeply in character for 10 years you didn't notice."[90]

show *At Home with Amy Sedaris.* "Paul [Dinello] and I have known Stephen since 1985 in *Strangers.* We can't do the show without having Colbert on it. And he plays himself because the part we had written for him, somebody has to play himself,"[1] Sedaris commented.

Colbert is shown here hosting the 69th Primetime Emmy Awards at the Microsoft Theater in Los Angeles, California.

Along with these appearances, Colbert has also been a leading man. In 2017, he hosted the 69th Primetime Emmy Awards in Los Angeles. With a spirited show tune number, Colbert opened what proved to be a very popular awards show.

1. Quoted in Jean Bentley, "'At Home with Amy Sedaris' Is a Comedy, but It's No Joke to Its Star and Creator," *The Hollywood Reporter*, October 23, 2017. www.hollywoodreporter.com/live-feed/at-home-amy-sedaris-is-a-comedy-but-no-joke-star-creator-1050999.

A Fresh Start

On September 8, 2015, Colbert opened his first show in late night as himself. The blustering clueless character of old was retired, and Colbert was free to show off his comedic chops and his depth as his true self. It did not take long for viewers to see the serious and deeply intelligent side of Colbert.

The Late Show follows a familiar format: It opens with a monologue about the day's news and has a celebrity interview and

Colbert officially took over as host of *The Late Show* on September 8, 2015.

musical guest. The changes in Colbert's interview style were noticeable from the first episode. Instead of playing a clownish character and often antagonizing his guests, Colbert had turned more serious, though he remained a comedian at heart. In a 2016 interview, Colbert said,

> *I used to interview people [in] character. And I had an agenda. I was going to win the interview. And it was fun to win it. Now, [I'm] myself, so I'm responsible for everything I'm saying and that—that made me sort of pull my natural punch in interviews for the first probably six months of the show.*[91]

It took about a year for Colbert to become comfortable with himself behind the *Late Show* desk after moving on from his *Colbert Report* persona.

Keeping Democracy Alive on TV

Throughout 2017, Colbert's run on *The Late Show* topped the ratings for late-night television. Many called him the new king of late night, but Colbert does not want to be king:

> *I have no interest in that, the whole realm. Johnny Carson [host of* The Tonight Show *from 1962 to 1992] was the last person who could say that. Because to be unchallenged is to be king, and there has been no one unchallenged since Johnny. And anyway, I'd much rather be the President of Late Night. If people want to vote, that's great. I'm an American. I don't want to be king of anything.*[1]

1. Quoted in Brian Steinbergh, "Stephen Colbert Q&A: Despite Politics, 'Late Show' Host Just Wants to Make Audiences Laugh," *Variety*, September 13, 2017. variety.com/2017/tv/news/stephen-colbert-late-show-interview-trump-cbs-1202556632/.

Not only had the interviewing style changed, but Colbert was now joined by a house band—Stay Human—led by Julliard-trained Jon Batiste. The show continues to be filmed in its long-time home, New York City's famed Ed Sullivan Theater.

At first, ratings were not great for the new show. *The Late Show* fell behind the shows of other late-night comedians. It seemed transitioning out of character was harder for Colbert than he had thought. Without the cover of his faux newsman persona, who was the real Stephen Colbert? It took about a year for the show to find its stride and for Colbert to find himself again. As the 2016 election season kicked into high gear, Colbert was able to bring some of his past political self to late night.

Perfect Timing

Colbert's entry into late-night network television could not have come at a better time for ratings success. After Jon Stewart left *The Daily Show* in 2015, a generation of TV viewers felt its source for news and political commentary had shifted. The new host of *The Daily Show*, Trevor Noah, had not yet gained the following and trust that Stewart had built. After the slow start transitioning from his *Colbert Report* persona back to himself, Colbert was able to capitalize on the timing of another presidential election and the void in political comedy. However, Colbert was still cautious:

Someone said to me the other day, you know, you keep on saying you guys have nothing to do with journalism, and well, I have enough people who disagree with you. And I said, "Well, I know they mean it as a compliment, but we are doing comedy. We just happen to be doing comedy about things that happened in the news today. That's how we found out about it." I'm a fan of the news. I like the news. But I'm in no way in competition with them. I don't want the status, or, I believe, the respect they deserve. I don't want any of that.[92]

When Donald J. Trump announced his run for president, many news shows and comedians did not take him seriously. By the time he won the presidency in November 2016, Colbert had turned the unprecedented election season into a ratings win. Some thought he focused too much on politics and on the Republican presidential nominee, but Colbert was clear in interviews: "I don't have an ax to grind. I get disappointed with both sides. But I do like human behavior. So that's what I enjoy talking about, and sometimes politics reflects human behavior. If I thought I had a political point, I'd be in big trouble."[93]

The head of CBS, Les Moonves, agreed that Colbert's take on politics was what Americans needed: "People want to see social commentary at the end of the night. They don't want to see fun and games."[94] Colbert has never lost sight of the comedy in politics.

Another part of the success of *The Late Show* was Colbert's decision to let go of the details. Unlike with *The Colbert Report*, where he had a hand in every aspect of running a show, by 2016 Colbert had let others step in. CBS hired a showrunner to focus on the details so Colbert could focus on being funny. Instead of worrying over the set or the guests, Colbert is now back to writing jokes and improvising. Without the burden of running the show, he has relaxed into late nights.

Late Nights Making Comedy Gold

Over the next few years, Colbert's reign on *The Late Show* continued to rise in the ratings. By 2017, *The Late Show* was beating other nightly comedy shows including *The Tonight Show with Jimmy Fallon*, *Jimmy Kimmel Live!*, and even *The Daily Show with Trevor Noah*. After the contentious 2016 election, Colbert and many other late-night show hosts became more political in their comedy. This proved to be great for *The Late Show*. It seemed audiences had missed Colbert's views on politicians and bombastic news.

Clips of Colbert's takes on President Trump constantly go viral. Some people feel this coverage is too much or too mean. However, the late shows have become more political in general over the years and have always reflected on the big news headlines. As Colbert has said, "When Trump's not the headline, we will do a joke on whatever the headline is, because the show is not about Donald Trump. The show is about what everyone is talking about today. This is the only thing anyone is talking about. Every day. *For the last year*."[95]

Jon Stewart made an appearance on *The Late Show* on November 8, 2017.

Honored by His Peers

The kudos that Colbert has received over the years are evidence of his popularity and recognition of his work. In 2006, *TIME* magazine named Colbert to its annual "*TIME* 100" list of the world's most influential people. The same year, *New York Magazine* named Colbert, along with Jon Stewart, one of the dozen most influential people in the media. Other media outlets have joined in, and in December 2007, the Associated Press named Colbert their Celebrity of the Year.

The Colbert Report received critical acclaim, winning the Emmy Award for Outstanding Writing in 2008, 2010, 2013, and 2014. Overall, Colbert has received 9 Emmy awards and 30 nominations over his career. *The Colbert Report* also received the Peabody Award for Excellence in Broadcasting in 2008 and 2012. As he accepted his Peabody in 2008, Colbert said in his usual deadpan, "I proudly accept this award and begrudgingly forgive the Peabody Committee for taking three years to recognize greatness."[1]

Other awards have acknowledged his *Colbert Report* persona. For example, in June 2008, the senior class of Princeton University presented its commencement speaker—Colbert—with "The Understandable Vanity Award," which consisted of a drawing and a mirror. Gazing into the mirror, Colbert raved in mock arrogance: "I've never seen anything more beautiful."[2]

1. Huffington Post, "Colbert Wins Peabody Award, Laughs in Jon Stewart's Face," April 11, 2008. www.huffingtonpost.com/2008/04/03/colbert-wins-peabody-awar_n_94820.html.

2. Quoted in "Class Day 2008," Princeton University. www.princeton.edu/pr/gradpics/2008/classday/index.htm.

Author Jonathan Franzen appeared on *The Late Show* on October 28, 2017, and read a bedtime story to Colbert.

Even though *The Late Show* tone tends toward the political, Colbert proves in other segments of the show that he still knows how to talk about other subjects. In the tradition of late-night shows, Colbert still interviews celebrities and artists. What sets *The Late Show* apart is Colbert's skits and improvised moments with his guests. One segment with then-vice-president Joe Biden showed "America's dad" giving advice to the nation. When Colbert has authors on the show, he has them read him bedtime stories.

In another segment, Colbert gives his "Midnight Confessions," poking fun at his devout Catholicism. In one confession, Colbert starts out, "Forgive me audience. I've been to confession more times on this show than I have in real life."[96] These confessions were made into a book in 2017.

Colbert Online and at Home

Colbert's tradition of getting the audience—and the Colbert Nation—involved in his work did not stop with the end of *The Colbert Report*. Since his first days on *The Late Show*, Colbert has been asking for audience participation. During regular episodes and sketches, the audience even has their own lines, such as telling Colbert he is forgiven during "Midnight Confessions."

Colbert keeps his audience engaged outside of the show, too. Through his personal Twitter account (@StephenAtHome), Colbert uses comedy to cover serious subjects. In 2017, he and comedian Nick Kroll started a hashtag called #PuberMe,

Physicist Neil deGrasse Tyson appeared on *The Late Show* with his #PuberMe photo.

which called for celebrities to tweet photos of themselves as awkward teenagers. Colbert vowed to donate $1,000 for every celebrity photo to help Puerto Rico recover from 2017's Hurricane Maria.

Celebrities from "Weird Al" Yankovic to *Hamilton* creator and star Lin-Manuel Miranda responded with their awkward photos. Donations were made from the Stephen Colbert Americone Dream Fund. The fund receives money from every purchase of Ben & Jerry's Americone Dream ice cream.

The #PuberMe challenge ended up raising $1 million for Puerto Rico. The money was donated to One America Appeal, a relief fund founded by the five living past presidents of the United States: Jimmy Carter, George H. W. Bush, George W. Bush, Bill Clinton, and Barack Obama.

Legacy of the Fool

As many reviewers of *The Colbert Report* have pointed out, American media analysts and politicians all seem to be in character; Colbert just made his character a bit more obvious. As satire, Colbert came so close to mocking the real deal that he was like the traditional fool to the king—getting the monarch to see his flaws by making fun of him in an exaggerated way. With *The Late Show*, Americans have continued to embrace the comedy and truth of America's fool. Colbert has said, "You know, I really love this job because I get to approach the terrible things that are happening in America with jokes."[97] Fans hope Colbert will continue to play the fool for years to come.

Colbert was named one of *GQ* magazine's "Men of the Year" in December 2017.

Notes

Introduction:
America's Comedic Voice

1. Quoted in Sophia A. McClennen, *Colbert's America: Satire and Democracy*. New York, NY: Palgrave Macmillan, 2011, p. 105.

2. Aaron Allen Schiller, ed., *Stephen Colbert and Philosophy: I Am Philosophy (And So Can You!)*. Chicago, IL: Open Court, 2009, p. xii.

Chapter One:
Joy from Sorrow

3. Quoted in "With Integrity and Dignity: The Life of James W. Colbert, Jr., MD," MUSC Library, 2011. waring.library.musc.edu/exhibits/colbert/Legacy. php.

4. Quoted in David Cote, "Joyce Words," *Time Out New York*, December 16, 2010. www.timeout.com/ newyork/film/joyce-words.

5. Quoted in Neil Strauss, "Stephen Colbert on Deconstructing the Colbert Nation," *Rolling Stone*, September 2, 2009. www.rollingstone.com/cul- ture/news/stephen-colbert-on-deconstructing-the- news-religion-and-the-colbert-nation-20090902.

6. Quoted in Deborah Solomon, "The Way We Live Now: 9-25-05: Questions for Stephen Colbert; Funny About the News," *New York Times*, September 25, 2005. query.nytimes.com/gst/fullpage.html?res =9C04E1DE1630F936A1575AC0A9639C8B63.

7. Quoted in Robin Finn, "Public Lives: Covering the Convention for Laughs," *New York Times*, August 27, 2004. www.nytimes.com/2004/08/27/nyregion/public-lives-covering-the-convention-for-laughs.html.

8. Quoted in Prentiss Findlay, "CBS Picks Charleston's Stephen Colbert to Succeed Letterman on 'Late Show,'" *Post and Courier*, April 9, 2014. www.postandcourier.com/archives/cbs-picks-charleston-s-stephen-colbert-to-succeed-letterman-on/article_94a5b228-bef1-5c50-8f70-b2e0545bb829.html.

9. Quoted in Daniel Schorn, "The Colbert Report," CBS News, April 27, 2006. www.cbsnews.com/stories/2006/04/27/60minutes/main1553506.shtml?tag=contentMain;content Body.

10. Quoted in Findlay, "CBS Picks Charleston's Stephen Colbert.'"

11. Quoted in James Kaplan, "If You Are Laughing, You Can't Be Afraid," *Parade*, September 23, 2007. web.archive.org/web/20100107022032/http:/www.parade.com/articles/editions/2007/edition_09-23-2007/AStephen_Colbert.

12. Quoted in Ken Plume, "An Interview with Stephen Colbert," IGN, August 11, 2003. www.ign.com/articles/2003/08/11/an-interview-with-stephen-colbert.

13. Quoted in Plume, "An Interview with Stephen Colbert."

14. Quoted in Plume, "An Interview with Stephen Colbert."

15. Quoted in Nathan Rabin, "Interview: Stephen Colbert," AV Club, January 25, 2006. www.avclub.com/articles/stephencolbert,13970/.

16. Quoted in Rabin, "Interview: Stephen Colbert."

17. Quoted in Cate Plys, "The Real Stephen Colbert," *Northwestern*, Winter 2010. www.northwestern.edu/magazine/winter2010/feature/the-real-stephen-colbert.html.

18. Quoted in Plys, "The Real Stephen Colbert."

19. Quoted in Plys, "The Real Stephen Colbert."

20. Quoted in Plys, "The Real Stephen Colbert."

21. Quoted in Plume, "An Interview with Stephen Colbert."

22. Paul Dinello, Amy Sedaris, and Randolph Heard, "A Burden's Burden," *Strangers with Candy*, season 1, episode 2, directed by Peter Lauer, aired April 14, 1999.

**Chapter Two:
A New Kind of Comedy**

23. Quoted in Plume, "An Interview with Stephen Colbert."

24. Quoted in Elana Berkowitz and Amy Schiller, "A Super Straight Guy," Alternet, July 28, 2005. www.alternet.org/story/23524/a_super_straight_guy.

25. Quoted in Plume, "An Interview with Stephen Colbert."

26. Quoted in Plume, "An Interview with Stephen Colbert."

27. Quoted in Lisa Rogak, *And Nothing but the Truthiness: The Rise (and Further Rise) of Stephen Colbert*. New York, NY: St. Martin's Press, 2011, p. 131.

28. "Klassic Kolbert—Civil Lights," *The Daily Show with Jon Stewart* video, 4:40, Comedy Central, February 8, 2006. www.cc.com/video-clips/v8phl0/the-daily-show-with-jon-stewart-klassic-kolbert---civil-lights.

29. Quoted in Berkowitz and Schiller, "A Super Straight Guy."

30. Quoted in Kaplan, "If You Are Laughing."

31. Quoted in Rogak, *And Nothing but the Truthiness*, p. 133.

32. Quoted in Rogak, *And Nothing but the Truthiness*, p. 158.

33. Quoted in Rogak, *And Nothing but the Truthiness*, p. 130.

34. Quoted in Finn, "Public Lives."

35. Quoted in Jake Coyle, "The 'Colbert Report' Behind the Scenes," *Huffington Post*, June 9, 2008. www.huffingtonpost.com/2008/06/09/the-colbert-report-behind_n_105988.html.

36. Quoted in Rogak, *And Nothing but the Truthiness*, p. 165.

Chapter Three:
The Importance of Truthiness

37. Quoted in Johnny Frohlichstein, "Pundit Face-Off: Stewart vs. Colbert," *Kirkwood Call*, April 20, 2011. www.thekirkwoodcall.com/opinion/2011/04/20/pundit-face-offstewart-vs-colbert/.

38. Quoted in Plys, "The Real Stephen Colbert."

39. Nancy Franklin, "The Spinoff Zone," *New Yorker*, November 28, 2005. www.newyorker.com/archive/2005/11/28/051128crte_television.

40. Quoted in Marc Peyser, "The Truthiness Teller," *Newsweek*, February 12, 2006. www.newsweek.com/2006/02/12/the-truthiness-teller.html.

41. Quoted in Jake Coyle, "Colbert's 'Report' Rapport Still Strong," *Seattle Times*, July 7, 2008. seattletimes.nwsource.com/html/television/2008035067_colbertreport07.html.

42. "The Word—Truthiness," *The Colbert Report* video, 2:40, Comedy Central, October 17, 2005. www.comedycentral.com.au/throwbacks/videos/the-colbert-report-the-very-first-episode-clips#the-word-truthiness.

43. Mark Peters, "Mark Peters on the Colbert Suffix," *Good Magazine*, October 3, 2007. www.good.is/post/mark-peters-on-the-colbert-suffix/.

44. "The Word—Truthiness," *The Colbert Report*.

45. Quoted in Adam Sternbergh, "Stephen Colbert Has America by the Ballots," *New York Magazine*, October 8, 2006. nymag.com/news/politics/22322/.

46. Quoted in James Klatell, "The Word of the Year: 'Truthiness,'" CBS News, December 9, 2006. www.cbsnews.com/news/the-word-of-the-year-truthiness/.

47. Quoted in Schiller, *Stephen Colbert and Philosophy*, p. 111.

48. Ben Zimmer, "Truthiness," *New York Times*, October 13, 2010. www.nytimes.com/2010/10/17/magazine/17FOBonlanguage-t.html.

49. Quoted in Sternbergh, "Stephen Colbert Has America by the Ballots."

50. Quoted in Sternbergh, "Stephen Colbert Has America by the Ballots."

51. "The Word—Truthiness," *The Colbert Report*.

52. Quoted in Plys, "The Real Stephen Colbert."

53. "The Word—Wikiality," *The Colbert Report* video, 4:10, Comedy Central, July 31, 2006. www.cc.com/video-clips/z1aahs/the-colbert-report-the-word---wikiality.

54. "The Word—Wikilobbying," *The Colbert Report* video, 3:18, Comedy Central, January 29, 2007. www.cc.com/video-clips/6p6df7/the-colbert-report-the-word---wikilobbying.

55. "The Word—Wikiality," *The Colbert Report*.

56. "The Word—Wikiality," *The Colbert Report.*

57. Quoted in Schiller, *Stephen Colbert and Philosophy*, p. 105.

58. "The Word—Truthiness," *The Colbert Report.*

59. Quoted in Schiller, *Stephen Colbert and Philosophy*, p. 69.

60. Sternbergh, "Stephen Colbert Has America by the Ballots."

61. "Better Know a District—Virginia's 3rd," *The Colbert Report* video, 8:00, Comedy Central, May 5, 2014. www.cc.com/video-clips/0hu2aq/the-colbert-report-better-know-a-district---virginia-s-3rd.

62. "Better Know a Founder—Thomas Jefferson," *The Colbert Report* video, 7:10, Comedy Central, November 15, 2006. www.cc.com/video-clips/47a505/the-colbert-report-better-know-a-founder---thomas-jefferson.

63. Steven Daly, "Stephen Colbert: The Second Most Powerful Idiot in America," *Telegraph*, May 18, 2008. www.telegraph.co.uk/culture/theatre/4205284/Stephen-Colbert-the-second-most-powerful-idiot-in-America.html.

64. Quoted in Daly, "Stephen Colbert."

65. Quoted in Plys, "The Real Stephen Colbert."

66. Quoted in Seth Mnookin, "The Man in the Irony Mask," *Vanity Fair*, September 24, 2007. www.vanityfair.com/culture/features/2007/10/colbert200710.

Chapter Four:
Changing Politics and Giving Back

67. Quoted in Jacques Steinberg, "After Press Dinner, the Blogosphere Is Alive with the Sound of Colbert Chatter," *New York Times*, May 3, 2006. www.nytimes.com/2006/05/03/arts/03colb.html.

68. Quoted in Sternbergh, "Stephen Colbert Has America by the Ballots."

69. Quoted in Sternbergh, "Stephen Colbert Has America by the Ballots."

70. Quoted in Sternbergh, "Stephen Colbert Has America by the Ballots."

71. Frank Rich, "Throw the Truthiness Bums Out," *New York Times*, November 5, 2006. select.nytimes.com/2006/11/05/opinion/05rich.html.

72. Quoted in Sternbergh, "Stephen Colbert Has America by the Ballots."

73. Quoted in James Poniewozik, "Stephen Colbert and the Death of 'The Room,'" Tuned In, *TIME*, May 3, 2006. tunedin.blogs.time.com/2006/05/03/stephen_colbert_and_the_death/.

74. Quoted in Strauss, "Stephen Colbert on Deconstructing the Colbert Nation."

75. Maureen Dowd and Stephen Colbert, "A Mock Columnist, Amok," *New York Times*, October 14, 2007. www.nytimes.com/2007/10/14/opinion/14dowd.html.

76. Quoted in Daniel Kurtzman, "Best Stephen Colbert Quotes," ThoughtCo., March 18, 2017. www.thoughtco.com/best-stephen-colbert-quotes-2734729.

77. Quoted in Tom Baldwin, "Making the Campaign into a Running Joke," *Times* (London), October 27, 2007. www.timesonline.co.uk/tol/news/world/us_and_americas/article2748888.ece.

78. Quoted in Rachel Sklar, "Colbert—and His Wife—Rock the New Yorker Fest," *Huffington Post*, October 6, 2008. www.huffingtonpost.com/2008/10/06/stephen-colbert-at-the-em_n_132019.html.

79. Quoted in "Thousands Expected at Stewart-Colbert Rally in DC," ABC News, October 29, 2010. abc7news.com/archive/7755467/.

80. Quoted in Zimmer, "Truthiness."

81. Quoted in Lisa de Moraes, "Answering Beck and Call? Jon Stewart, Stephen Colbert Head to the Mall," *Washington Post*, September 18, 2010. www.washingtonpost.com/wp-dyn/content/article/2010/09/17/AR2010091706751.html.

82. Quoted in Moraes, "Answering Beck and Call?"

83. Quoted in Daniel Kurtzman, "The Funniest Signs at the Rally to Restore Sanity and/or Fear," ThoughtCo., September 1, 2017. www.thoughtco.com/signs-rally-to-restore-sanity-fear-4122837.

84. Jon Stewart, "Keynote Address at the Rally to Restore Sanity," American Rhetoric, October 30,

2010. www.americanrhetoric.com/speeches/jon-stewartsanityrallykeynote.htm.

85. Stewart, "Keynote Address."

86. Quoted in Peter Grier, "Stephen Colbert on Capitol Hill: Did He Help Migrant Workers?," *Christian Science Monitor*, September 24, 2010. www.csmonitor.com/USA/Elections/Vox-News/2010/0924/Stephen-Colbert-on-Capitol-Hill-Did-he-help-migrant-workers.

87. Grier, "Stephen Colbert on Capitol Hill."

Chapter Five:
A Leader in Late Night

88. Quoted in "'Late Show' Host Says He Has Finally Found His Post-'Colbert Report' Voice," Fresh Air with Terry Gross, NPR, November 2, 2016. www.npr.org/2016/11/02/500303201/late-show-host-stephen-colbert-says-hes-finally-found-his-post-report-voice.

89. Quoted in Brian Steinbergh, "Stephen Colbert Q&A: Despite Politics, 'Late Show' Host Just Wants to Make Audiences Laugh," *Variety*, September 13, 2017. variety.com/2017/tv/news/stephen-colbert-late-show-interview-trump-cbs-1202556632/.

90. Quoted in Jen Yamato, "Stephen Colbert on Dropping 'The Colbert Report' Persona and the Glorious Debut of 'The Colbeard,'" *Daily Beast*, February 20, 2015. www.thedailybeast.com/stephen-colbert-on-dropping-the-colbert-report-persona-and-the-glorious-debut-of-the-colbeard.

91. Quoted on "Face the Nation: Colbert, CBS Correspondents Roundtable," CBS News, December 25, 2016. www.cbsnews.com/news/face-the-nation-transcript-december-25-2016-colbert-correspondents-panel/.

92. Quoted in Steinbergh, "Stephen Colbert Q&A."

93. Quoted in Neil Strauss, "Colbert Show: The Subversive Joy of Stephen Colbert," *Rolling Stone*, September 17, 2009. www.rollingstone.com/movies/news/the-subversive-joy-of-stephen-colbert-20090917.

94. Quoted in Josef Adalian, "How Stephen Colbert Got His Groove Back," Vulture, March 13, 2017. www.vulture.com/2017/03/stephen-colbert-how-he-got-his-groove-back.html.

95. Quoted in Steinbergh, "Stephen Colbert Q&A."

96. "The Best of Stephen Colbert's Midnight Confessions," YouTube video, 3:04, posted by *The Late Show with Stephen Colbert*, April 10, 2017. www.youtube.com/watch?v=8SeW0ge-7LA.

97. Quoted in Steinbergh, "Stephen Colbert Q&A."

Stephen Colbert Year by Year

1964

Stephen Colbert is born on May 13, 1964.

1974

Colbert's father and two brothers are killed in an airplane crash.

1982

Colbert enrolls in the all-male Hampden-Sydney College in Virginia.

1984

Colbert transfers to Northwestern University's School of Communication as a theater major and begins performing improvisation with the No Fun Mud Piranhas (the campus improvisation team) and at the Annoyance Theater in Chicago.

1986

Colbert graduates from Northwestern University

1987

Colbert takes a job selling tickets for The Second City in Chicago, Illinois.

1991

Colbert begins performing at Second City Northwest.

1995

Colbert develops *Exit 57*, a comedy sketch show that runs on Comedy Central.

1996

Colbert works briefly as a cast member and writer on *The Dana Carvey Show* and as a freelance writer for *Saturday Night Live*.

1997

Colbert joins the cast of *The Daily Show* as a correspondent character.

1999

Colbert develops and performs in *Strangers with Candy*, a comedy series picked up by Comedy Central.

2000

Colbert covers the presidential election season as part of *The Daily Show*'s award-winning coverage and performs voice-over work for the Cartoon Network animated series *Harvey Birdman, Attorney at Law*.

2003

Colbert coauthors the satirical novel *Wigfield: The Can-Do Town That Just May Not*.

2004

Along with the cast of *The Daily Show*, Colbert covers the presidential election and shares the Emmy Award for Outstanding Writing for a Variety, Music or Comedy Program with *The Daily Show*.

2005

Colbert hosts *The Colbert Report* on Comedy Central; appears in a film adaptation of *Strangers with Candy*; appears in a supporting role in the movie *Bewitched*; and receives a second Emmy Award for writing on *The Daily Show*.

2006

Colbert gives a much-publicized keynote speech at the White House Correspondents' Association dinner and wins a third Emmy Award for writing on *The Daily Show*; Merriam-Webster names "truthiness" its 2005 Word of the Year; *TIME* names Colbert to its *TIME* 100 list of the world's most influential people; and Colbert receives an honorary doctorate in fine arts from Knox College in Illinois.

2007

Ben & Jerry's releases a new ice cream flavor, Stephen Colbert's Americone Dream; Colbert announces his presidential candidacy in October; in November, the South Carolina Democratic Party votes to keep Colbert's name off the ballot; Colbert publishes the satirical book *I Am America (And So Can You!)*; and the Associated Press names Colbert Celebrity of the Year.

2008

Colbert receives a Peabody Award for *The Colbert Report*; he receives an Emmy Award for writing for *The Colbert Report*; and his Christmas special, *A Colbert Christmas: The Greatest Gift of All!* airs on Comedy Central and is later released to DVD.

2009

Under the guise "Operation Iraqi Stephen: Going Commando," Colbert tapes a week's worth of episodes for *The Colbert Show* at Camp Victory in Baghdad, Iraq; the commander of U.S. forces in Iraq shaves Colbert's head as part of the routine; and Colbert signs a sponsorship agreement with the U.S. Olympic speed skating team after the team loses a prominent sponsor.

2010

Colbert participates in the United Farm Workers' "Take Our Jobs" program, during which he spends a day picking vegetables with migrant farm workers; he later testifies on behalf of migrant workers before a House subcommittee on Capitol Hill in Washington, D.C.; he receives a Grammy Award for Best Comedy Album for *A Colbert Christmas: The Greatest Gift of All!*; and along with Jon Stewart, he hosts the Rally to Restore Sanity and/or Fear in Washington, D.C.

2011

Colbert files papers to launch his own political action committee to draw attention to campaign finance laws and joins a Charleston-to-Bermuda yachting race as honorary captain of the sailboat *Spirit of Juno*, finishing second.

2013

Colbert's mother, Lorna, dies at the age of 92 on June 12, and Colbert takes a break from his show and returns with a touching eulogy.

2014

Colbert hosts his first awards show, *The Kennedy Center Honors*. These lifetime achievement awards are given to those who have made substantial contributions to the performing arts. Colbert would go on to host the 2015 and 2016 awards as well. Colbert closes down *The Colbert Report* with its last episode on December 18.

2015

Colbert replaces David Letterman on *The Late Show* on CBS and receives the Outstanding Civilian Service Award from the U.S. Army.

2017

Colbert's *The Late Show* leads the ratings in late-night television; Colbert again becomes a strong voice in American politics; and Colbert hosts the 69th Primetime Emmy Awards in Los Angeles, California.

For More Information

Books

Aldridge, Rebecca. *Stephen Colbert*. New York, NY: Rosen Publishing, 2016.
Readers learn about Stephen Colbert's rise to fame and the ways his shows have affected American culture.

Andronik, Catherine M. *Stephen Colbert: A Biography*. Santa Barbara, CA: Greenwood, 2012.
This book examines the impact of Stephen Colbert's comedic take on American culture.

Rogak, Lisa. *And Nothing but the Truthiness: The Rise (and Further Rise) of Stephen Colbert*. New York, NY: St. Martin's Press, 2012.
Learn more about the star of *The Colbert Report* and his rise to fame in this informative and entertaining book.

Schiller, Aaron Allen, ed. *Stephen Colbert and Philosophy: I Am Philosophy (And So Can You!)*. Chicago, IL: Open Court, 2009.
This collection of essays explains the comedy of Stephen Colbert.

Watson, Bruce. *Stephen Colbert: Beyond Truthiness*. Newbury, MA: New Word City, LLC, 2016.
This book follows Stephen Colbert on his rise to comedic fame.

Websites

The Colbert Report
(www.cc.com/shows/the-colbert-report)
This website is an archive of *The Colbert Report* on Comedy Central.
  The website includes a searchable archive of video clips from
  Colbert's debut show to the final episode, as well as highlights
  and full episodes.

The Daily Show with Jon Stewart
(www.cc.com/shows/the-daily-show-with-jon-stewart)
The official home of *The Daily Show with Jon Stewart* online
  includes a searchable archive of video clips that feature Stephen
  Colbert as a correspondent and as a character in other skits.

Facebook: The Late Show with Stephen Colbert
(www.facebook.com/colbertlateshow/)
The official Facebook page for *The Late Show with Stephen Colbert*,
  this website provides the latest information about Colbert and
  The Late Show.

The Late Show with Stephen Colbert
(www.cbs.com/shows/the-late-show-with-stephen-colbert/)
This is the official CBS website of *The Late Show with Stephen
  Colbert*. Includes clips of popular monologues, skits,
  and interviews.

Stephen Colbert
(www.imdb.com/name/nm0170306/)
The International Movie Database keeps track of Stephen Colbert's
  filmography, awards, and more.

Twitter: Stephen Colbert
(twitter.com/StephenAtHome)
Colbert's official Twitter page is frequently updated with jokes and
  videos from *The Late Show with Stephen Colbert*.

Index

Picture Credits

About the Author

Allison Krumsiek is an author and poet living in Washington, D.C. She writes for a number of organizations, including nonprofits and the federal government, and also authors nonfiction books for young adults. When she isn't writing or editing, Allison can be found reading books or fearlessly defending her field hockey goal, but never at the same time.